Advance Praise for *Sheep No More*

"Jonathan Gilliam's unique Attack and Defend system is the cutting edge of personal and administrative safety in the age of terrorism. He's unafraid to spotlight uncomfortable truths, yet the system is a positive, proactive plan for identifying, preventing, and avoiding everything from ordinary street crime to major acts of terrorism. The case studies alone, about how real people behaved in real situations, are worth the price of the book."

—MARCUS LUTTRELL, former Navy SEAL, awarded the Navy Cross and Purple Heart; author of *Lone Survivor*

"Given the depth of his training and field it is no surprise that Jonathan Gilliam commands widespread respect across the nation as an expert in threat assessment, evaluation, and response. When the bad guys strike, he's the guy you want in the foxhole with you or, better still, designing your foxhole and the strategy of its defense."

—PAUL CALLAN, CNN legal analyst, former New York City homicide prosecutor, media law professor

"Jonathan Gilliam and I served together in the SEAL Teams. His proven experience as a military warrior combined with his time as an FBI agent gives him an enhanced technical knowledge and worldview perspective that is perfect for providing risk assessment of current events, as well as threats to our national security. Jonathan's Attack and Defend technique provides an in-depth analytical skillset for the untrained civilian so they, too, can fully develop their understanding of current threats and how to defend against them."

—DRAGO, U.S. Navy SEAL (retired)

"Jonathan brings a combination of actual tactical and strategic experience to provide better analysis and further, a more in-depth discussion of complex and evolving issues."

—DAVID WEBB, host of *The David Webb Show*, Fox News contributor

"I can heartily recommend anything that my friend Jonathan Gilliam writes! His take on what confronts us in *Sheep No More* will resonate with ALL interested Americans, written in the wry style that we have grown to expect of Jonathan in his numerous television and radio appearances!"

—SCOTT UEHLINGER, CIA Station Chief, (retired) naval officer

"Having spent 33 years in the U.S. Army, and being a mother to 2 children who now defend our freedoms in active duty military roles, I know the importance of awareness. *Sheep No More* takes the technical information used to identify and target an enemy and disseminates it in a way everyday Americans can understand. Get this book, read it, and put the technique of Attack and Defend to work in your life."

—KITTY KELLY, Sergeant Major, U.S. Army (retired)

"*Sheep No More* shows a sharp in-depth knowledge of the hidden dangers that surround us in an ever-changing threat scenario. Jonathan's critical analysis of awareness leads to a lifesaving response and/or avoidance."

—DR. WALLY GRAND, neurosurgeon

"Jonathan Gilliam conveys a relentless and determined attitude to be the best, and his vigorous demeanor to all is unparalleled. Jonathan's warrior mindset and his accurate display of tactics, techniques, and procedures have proven to be invaluable over his extraordinary career."

—LENNY DEPAUL, Chief Inspector/Commander, U.S. Marshal Service (retired)

"While Jonathan and I rarely agree on politics, I am always impressed by his commitment to making his country better and helping people be aware of the dangers that exist in the modern world. For those looking to know more about these issues, *Sheep No More* will surely help to round out your view."

—RICK UNGAR, host of *The Steele and Ungar Show*

"As a former law enforcement officer, firearm instructor, and mother of 2, I have tried to utilize my knowledge and experience of ways I could protect my family. *Sheep No More* will open your mind up to a new way of thinking that allows you to better protect yourself, your family, and your home. This book is a must-read for anyone who wants to be in better control of their life and their personal safety."

—LIZ HUMBERT, mom, former police officer

"Jonathan's Attack and Defend technique reflects the very same techniques law enforcement uses to track bad guys and enhance our own force protection. Having operated with Jonathan on the street during arrests as part of the FBI/NYPD Criminal Task Force, I can tell you *Sheep No More* is the real deal and it will change the way you protect yourself and your family!"

—DORIS GARCIA, former NYPD police officer,
former FBI Operations Specialist

"Having worked with Jonathan in the SEAL Teams as well as collaborating on projects in the civilian world, I can truly say that his ability to make technical information understandable is second to none. I believe in his Attack and Defend technique found in *Sheep No More* that directly reflects the warrior's unconventional mindset. It is long overdue in the civilian world."

—MARC LONERGAN-HERTEL, former SEAL sniper,
author of *Sierra Two: A SEAL's Odyssey in War and Peace*

"Jonathan T. Gilliam doesn't stop when he's tired. He stops when he's done. His training has taught him to be excellent. Jonathan is an exceptional American and a patriot. Every American should read *Sheep No More*."

—JASON D. MEISTER, managing director
Real Estate Capital Advisor

THE ART OF AWARENESS AND ATTACK SURVIVAL

JONATHAN T. GILLIAM

FOREWORD BY SEAN HANNITY

A POST HILL PRESS BOOK

Sheep No More
The Art of Awareness and Attack Survival
© 2017 by Jonathan T. Gilliam
All Rights Reserved

ISBN: 978-1-68261-604-8
ISBN (eBook): 978-1-68261-605-5

Cover art by Quincy Avilio
Cover Photo by Barry Morgenstein Photography, barrymorgenstein.com
Interior Design and Composition, Greg Johnson/Textbook Perfect

Post Hill Press
New York • Nashville
posthillpress.com
Published in the United States of America

Dedication

Dedicated to the men and women who raise their right hands in support and defense of our Constitution at home and abroad, the military veterans, law-enforcement officers, intelligence operatives, contractors, and all those in an official capacity who keep our nation safe. May this book empower our citizenry to be a force multiplier in your fight against evil.

To my mother, to Christine, to my family and friends, and to the Grand family: Each one of you has assisted in one way or another in this gift of awareness I now give to the world so that it may be safer.

To all those who mentored me (John Crouch, Wally Grand, Jim Grindstaff, Ron Bellan, Sean Hannity, Lynda McLaughlin, Rick Ungar, and David Webb, just to name a few): Those who told me to shut up and listen, then asked my opinion once I gained the knowledge, understanding, and experience I needed—thank you for your patience and guidance.

To Rico and Jesse, my dogs: You helped me see the world from a different perspective, and brought light where there was darkness.

And yet we must acknowledge the one true God and His son, Jesus, for giving us history's greatest example of the sacrifice for the greater good of others. Your plan forged me so that others may know. Amen.

Table of Contents

Acknowledgments

SPECIAL THANKS TO MY publisher, Anthony Ziccardi, and the team at Post Hill Press, Billie Brownell and Michael L. Wilson, for guiding me and giving me the opportunity to empower our citizenry and make our homeland safer! One Team, One Fight!

Thank you to Jon Ford for your edits and guidance. Now I know why people pay big bucks for a quality editor.

Thank you to Jennifer Cohen for connecting the dots and finding the right publisher for this book.

Thank you to photographer Barry Morgenstein and makeup/artist/psychologist/angel Maureen Walsh for the incredible cover photos and support. You both are amazing, patriotic Americans!

To all those that assisted in editing and critiquing my manuscript (Salpi, Chris, Liz, Natalie, Jennifer, Jessica, and the Neumayers): your suggestions and devoted time made this possible, thank you!

Thank you, Sean Hannity, for being a great American, for giving me the opportunity to fill in on your show in your absence, and for writing the foreword to *Sheep No More*.

Thank you to all the men and women with whom I served at AMTI, where warriors went to do profound things.

ACKNOWLEDGMENTS

Thank you to the men and women of the NYPD for teaching me how to be a cop on the street.

A very, very special thanks to Kirby Scott, Debbie Bretshneider, and J. Kincaid, three of the finest leaders with whom I worked in the FBI, as well as Krista LNU, Jo LNU, and Rita LNU for the greatest support in the bureau.

Thank you to FNU LNU for keeping all the agents and detectives on their toes throughout the years. You have proven to be a worthy opponent.

Lastly, thank you to all the members of the #CQRF. I stand with you all!

Foreword

JONATHAN AND I MET several years ago on the set of my show on Fox News. He had, at that time, recently left the FBI and was quickly becoming a sought-after expert in media. He brought a multifaceted approach to national security, military, and law enforcement issue analysis with his varied background.

Since then, Jonathan has continued to define himself as an outside-the-box thinker. Specifically, Jonathan has appeared both on my television and radio shows championing the importance of awareness and attack avoidance, a subject that is largely missed by the rapidly changing news cycle.

In *Sheep No More,* Jonathan explains the subjective nature of self-defense. I have learned that throughout my years of training both with a concealed handgun and also through mixed martial arts, there are so many ways to approach self-defense, and most people tend to overlook awareness as the first step. This should be *standard operating procedure* and incorporated into every aspect of your life.

Since I began training in traditional fighting, my awareness on where and when an altercation could occur has increased. I saw a direct correlation between my awareness and the techniques I was learning. What I didn't realize however is that the way I was starting to see things was not from my own point of view, but from the point of view of someone that may want to do me, or my family, harm. This was an important turning point in my understanding of true self-defense. My actions became more focused and calculated. It's not just where and when an attack could happen, but also *who* might attack and *why* they would be focused on me.

Being a father, I have seen how important it is not only to know how to protect myself, but also my family. It's a driving force behind my training. Now I have realized how important it is for my children to learn to be aware of real world threats around them so they can avoid trouble all together, and if caught up in it, make the right decisions to act, not just react. *Sheep No More* teaches both sides of the potential event, and I could see these tactics being incorporated into schools, entertainment facilities, and so on where families could be spending time.

Sheep No More is a simple book that will alter your perception of understanding threats in the world around you. It is a book that empowers the reader with simple techniques to look at all aspects of their lives from an attacker's point of view in order to better secure your daily life. To my knowledge there has never been another book written that emphasizes the everyday citizens ability to understand how an attacker thinks, and then goes a step further by actually helping you understand and utilize the same techniques bad guys will use to collect information on you for the purpose of attacking you.

Sheep No More takes this same concept in mind and incorporates it into simple, everyday language. It's not the jargon of military and law enforcement experts. Nothing I have ever read has dared to broach the technique of teaching people how they can see themselves from the potential attacker's point of view; yet at the same time it is a technique that most of us have always performed on a subconscious level.

As a kid, asking myself "what if" was always the first thing I did if I was doing something on my own. Now, as an adult, I find myself asking that question again and again as I have more to lose. With *Sheep No More*, I have a more professional set of techniques to answer the question "what if"—it outlines the who, why, where, when, and how an attack may happen.

I hope you read this book, and then read it again to incorporate the techniques. It will transform the way you see self-defense. And remember, in order to be a great American, you have to be an alert and safe American, so stay aware and stay alive!

Sean Hannity

pred·a·tor

/ˈpredator/

Noun: **predator**; plural noun: **predators**

    1. An animal that naturally preys on others.

    2. A person or group that ruthlessly exploits others.

prey

prā/

Noun: **prey**

    1. An animal that is hunted and/or killed by another for food or control.

Introduction

Warning: This Book Will Change the Way You See the World

For a moment I want you to pause, and with a clear mind, I want you to read the following question and consider the implications of what it is asking you. *How much of your life, your safety, your awareness, your health, your learning, your relationship with God, the safety of your children, your money, and so on, how much of all that and the rest of your life depends upon protection from others?*

Not knowing the answers to this question is called learned helplessness, and wherever you see it, you will also see a cultural cancer of unawareness. Who protects your life? Who hates you? What are the tactics that those who protect you might use to ensure absolute survivability in something like a terrorist attack? Can you really plan and rehearse your actions if you are caught up in a violent attack? How do you know the tactics that bad guys will utilize to attack you? If you don't know the answers to these questions, then there is a good chance you have been indoctrinated to believe it's impossible for you to develop awareness and for you to be your own protector. That stops today!

Sheep No More is the awareness bible that allows you, the reader, to radically change your perception of the world around you, by teaching you proven techniques to discover the key criticalities of awareness in and around your surroundings. After reading this book, you will be able to make educated predictions about who and why you could be attacked, where and when attacks could happen, and how an attack could be carried out against you.

The key factor in this book is the technique of "Attack and Defend," which is based on a combination of tactics, techniques, and procedures I learned in the SEAL Teams and various law-enforcement agencies in which I served, combined with the simple "what if" game you might have played as a child.

The secret to gaining defensive awareness is first understanding how an attacker views potential targets. Without the knowledge of how an attacker thinks or a complete understanding of an attacker's target package, your ability to set up proper defenses is reduced to a guessing game. As you will see, the technique of Attack and Defend is dependent on a crawl, walk, run approach to gaining knowledge, then understanding, followed by experience in going back and forth between the attacker and defender mindset. In doing this, you reinforce your ability to combine the attacker and defender mindsets into one set of techniques so you can make educated decisions about your specific defensive critical areas, critical times, and vulnerabilities that make you susceptible to attack.

The chapters in *Sheep No More* are organized to guide you through a similar learning process as military and government targeting experts. First, you will learn the steps to build a target package. Next, you will learn how to analyze your life and its critical areas, critical times, vulnerabilities, and any avenues of approach, all from the attacker's point of view. This book will guide you through the various ways to collect information about yourself and your surroundings so you have a greater historical knowledge to defend against the different people and groups that might attack you, how their methods of attack have evolved, where their attacks have occurred, and when you are most likely to be attacked in your daily life.

As you develop an understanding of the attacker mindset and how they build a target package on the person, place, or thing they wish to attack, you will also develop a better understanding of how military and law-enforcement professionals plan their defenses in high-threat areas. Military and law-enforcement force protection defenses always encompass an understanding of both an attacker's and defender's mindset. As it has been shown in terrorist planning cycles, the information in an attacker's target package to determine how, when, where, and why they will attack is nearly identical to the information in an official threat assessment used to set up advanced defenses in and around government installations. Even the United States Secret Service considers as much as they can about an attacker's angle when they set out to protect the President of the United States.

Utilizing this awareness is how defensive measures are thought out, but it is also how responses to attacks themselves are created. Remember this: Even the greatest defenses and awareness cannot protect you 100-percent against possible attacks. As such, responses do not have to be reactive or based on instinctual reactions alone; they can be planned in advance if you know who, why, where, when, and how attacks could occur. As you learn the techniques of this book, you will begin to understand how to flip a switch from an offensive (attacker) mindset to a defensive (defender) mindset so that you can constantly activate your defenses and planned responses to an attack, both consciously and subconsciously.

The two faces on the cover of *Sheep No More* represent the two mindsets that have been cultivated inside me through years of my military and law enforcement career. On the left is the dark, unconventional attacker mindset and on the right is the professional, defender persona. As you will see, the potential to cultivate the attacker and defender mindsets that exists within you is absolutely possible, as both utilize the same collection of information to either build a defensive or offensive target package.

Most humans, unlike animal prey, fail to realize that in order to truly protect yourself, you must apply the knowledge the attacker has on you in order to gain well-rounded awareness, proper defenses, and adequate responses to actual attacks. Animals on the plains of Africa do not simply react to fear, as inexperienced "experts" would have you believe. Instead, prey animals that live daily under intense threats from larger, faster predators develop an understanding of which areas around them are critically dangerous, the critical times those areas present the biggest threat, and the location and direction for tactical avenues of approach a predator will likely take when they attack. These prey animals also have an in-depth, instinctual understanding of who the attackers are and what their own vulnerabilities are compared to their enemies' strengths. They are constantly learning from their parents and through their own experiences, then applying it to their overall knowledge of defense and responsive actions, just as the attackers utilize their own taught and learned knowledge and expertise in an offensive manner on a daily basis. In this tug of war between predators and prey on the plains of Africa, predators use their knowledge of the prey's daily life to exploit vulnerabilities, and the prey use the exact same knowledge to stay one step ahead of the cunning attackers.

This understanding is the essence of offensive/defensive warfare and it is how small units such as Navy SEALs can accomplish missions with crippling effects on larger forces, and it's how the U.S. government can stick an outpost in the middle of a war zone and still remain relatively safe. SEALs understand that in order to carry out an effective attack and remain alive, they must know as much as possible about the enemy and the target surroundings by performing target analysis. SEALs don't just "wing it" and use instinctual intuition to get them through the dangerous areas. The same goes for force protection threat assessments that determine the security setup for federal, state, and local military and law-enforcement installations. Both the force protection experts setting up defenses and the Navy SEAL operators setting up an offensive (attack) mission will first start their planning stages by gathering intelligence and creating a target package, just like the predator and prey in Africa. This target package tells the SEAL operators and the force protection experts how, when, where, and why the enemy or the installation is most vulnerable. That is what the techniques in *Sheep No More* are all about!

Consider how you already use these Attack and Defend tactics in your daily life without even realizing it. When you send your child off to martial arts training or baseball practice, they are learning basic awareness techniques. Most likely you already know these techniques too, and *Sheep No More* will help you understand how they can be used effortlessly in everyday life.

The martial arts teach a set of skills gathered from years of trial and error of encounters between opponents. Their moves are calculated, smooth, trained responses based on the predictive actions of the other fighter, not simply learning to react to the opponent's actions. In other words, these offensive and defensive skills are ingrained into a fighter's techniques, allowing for educated actions to confront their opponent in a predictive manner as compared to simply reacting in an unplanned fashion. In the practice of martial arts, the more understanding you have of your opponent's skills and tactics, the stronger and more effective your awareness and defenses will be.

Likewise, baseball teams practice defense with calculated, predictive, basic skills. Teams train to understand how to defend against what their opponents can or will do. For example, if the offensive batter is right-handed, the defensive outfield moves to a particular formation. If the batter swings with a dominant left hand, the defensive outfield predictively changes their formation to accommodate what they think will be the most probable area the ball will travel. Having served more than twenty years as a United States Navy SEAL officer, Federal Air Marshal (FAM), FBI Special Agent, police officer, crisis manager, and personal protection operator, I have honed the skills of targeting and threat-mitigation. I have had the opportunity to work closely with the public and private sectors as a government security expert and as the FBI special events coordinator for the New York office of the FBI's Joint Terrorism Task Force and Crisis Management Unit. As I worked in these positions, I not only saw a tremendous gap between security awareness for private sector venues and local, state, and federal agencies, but an even greater, almost immeasurable gap between government personnel and the civilian population.

All of these examples of prey and predator, offense and defense, and attacker and defender come down to three particular words: knowledge, understanding, and experience! The more you know, the more you understand what you know, and the more you apply it in real life, the more successful you will be at understanding who, why, when, where, and how you could be attacked and, in most cases, the more successful you will be at avoiding an attack all together.

What *Sheep No More* Is Not!

Sheep No More is *not* a handbook for attackers, nor is it simply a book of case studies and suggestions, as is the case with most books in this genre. As the old saying goes, if I teach you to fish, you will never go hungry. What you are about to learn, if applied, will greatly decrease the chance of you walking blindly into an attacker's web for the rest of your life! *Sheep No More* was not written with the professional special forces operator or the tactical gurus out there in mind. It's simplified so the average person can see a clear vision of the Attack and Defend technique of thinking like an attacker so that you can foresee who, why, where, when, and how someone would attack you where you live, work, and relax. I did not leave the operators completely out, however, because *Sheep No More* is a great book to gift to government officials and law-enforcement executives who are interested in expanding their knowledge of security matters but who may have risen through the ranks with a more administrative outlook on tactical operations and planning.

INTRODUCTION

Many of the facts in *Sheep No More* are harsh, but they are also eye-openers and keys to a safer future. Although it is not my intent as an expert to place blame and point fingers in all the case studies included in this book, I do find it necessary to point out that we have an epidemic of unawareness in this country. My mission and the mission of Attack and Defend is to cure that epidemic by teaching simple but effective techniques to everyone that will make life-saving changes in the way, we as a country, secure our homeland.

Key Terms

Attack: An aggressive and violent action against a person, place, or enemy force.

Attack and Defend: The back and forth technique of defending a person, place, or thing through the development of an attacker's mindset and utilizing it to gain target information that is compiled into an attacker's target package, which leads to awareness and attack avoidance.

Attacker: A person or animal that attacks someone or something.

Attacker's Avenue of Approach: An air or ground route of an attacking force leading to its objective.

Attack Possibility: Statistical calculations that reduce the likelihood of an attack to either yes or no.

Attack Probability: Statistical calculations that rate the most likely place for an attack by assigning a number percentage.

Awareness: Knowledge or perception of a situation or fact.

Criminal: A person who has committed illegal activity.

Critical Area: Soft target areas considered to have a heightened threat and easy access for an attacker.

Critical Asset: Facilities, systems, and equipment which, if destroyed, degraded, or otherwise rendered unavailable, would affect the reliability or operability of operations.

Criticalities: The five specific parts of a target (including Critical Assets, Critical Areas, Critical Times, Vulnerabilities, and Attackers' Avenues of Approach) comprised of the exploitable information sought after and utilized by attackers to build a target package and used by defenders to ensure proper defenses.

Critical Time: Specific times when a critical area is under the highest threat.

Defender: A person or animal attempting to ward off attack from an attacker.

Defense: The action of defending from or resisting attack.

Deranged: Mad; insane.

Hard Target: A building, facility, or area (critical area) that has been secured, making it less likely to be attacked.

Plan of Attack: Ideas or actions intended to deal with a problem or situation.

Private Sector: The part of the economy involved with enterprise not controlled by the state.

Procedures: Established and approved order of actions.

Public Sector: The part of the economy concerned with providing various government services.

Shared Threats: Possible or probable attacks shared by multiple locations or people or threats that, if carried out as an attack, could affect other nontargeted locations or people.

Soft Target: A building, facility, or critical area that is difficult to protect.

Standard Operating Procedures: The standardization of tactics, techniques, and procedures into a step-by-step process for streamlined operations.

Strategy: The thinking process required to plan a change, course of action, or organization. Strategy defines, or outlines, desired goals and why you should go about achieving them.

Surveillance: Observation for the purpose of information collection. Can be carried out electronically, in vehicle, or on foot.

Tactics: The specific actions you take in implementing your strategy.

Tactics, Techniques, and Procedures (TTP): Particular standard operating procedures utilized by attacking forces.

Target Package: Information collected in order to develop an accurate picture of a given target for the purpose of attacking or defending.

Task Organization: The process of assigning operations, tasks, work in an organized fashion.

Techniques: The specific style or form used or applied to tactics.

Terrorism: The use of fear, intimidation, and violence in the pursuit of a political aim.

Terrorist: A person who carries out a terror attack, or facilitates who, why, when, where, and how it will occur.

VBIED: Acronym for vehicle-borne improvised explosive device.

Vulnerability: Identifiable areas of a location, facility, or person being exposed to the possibility of being attacked.

PART 1

THE ATTACKER

By and large, this book comes down to one simple technique that you will fully understand more and more as you flow through the pages. That technique is called Attack and Defend, and as I explained in the introduction, flipping the switch between an attacker mindset and a defender mindset is something we often do subconsciously by utilizing nature's signals of danger that are instinctually placed inside us by God's divine wisdom, similar to a cheat code used by avid gaming enthusiasts to gain an upper hand on their competitors. Although this is probably the most difficult part of Attack and Defend to harness, it is critical for you to at least understand that this part of the human psyche exists so that you can see the potential critical areas and critical times attractive to an attacker as well as the vulnerabilities they may exploit, and the avenues of approach they may take as they perform pre-attack surveillance and/or carry out the actual attack.

Understanding what the attacker mindset entails is not something that is often encouraged by society, as most people seem to perceive contemplating the motivation and planning of an attacker is either useless or just too dangerous to teach. In fact, this understanding is perhaps the most useful part of building true defenses, and contrary to what many may think, understanding the mind of an attacker will not turn you into a madman. Ultimately, learning how an attacker thinks and plans an attack, along with what an attack actually is, will broaden your own knowledge and understanding of where you could be victimized. Putting these pieces of the puzzle together is exactly how you build a target package, and it is what will lead you to greater awareness and the understanding needed to avoid violent encounters all together.

CHAPTER 1

What Is the Attacker Mindset?

You should understand that developing awareness by building a target package from an attacker's point of view could be one of the greatest ways to build defenses in and around your own life, work, agency, or social structure. Along with this new awareness of effective defenses comes a more effective foundation for standard operating procedures (SOPs) that are truly worth having. So often, governments, businesses, and individuals develop SOPs without thinking them through and in most cases things are just done because "that's the way it's always been done."

I have always disliked the phrase "perception is reality" because of how often it is used to justify unqualified people attaining high positions and power. Yet it fits this discussion perfectly because the way you perceive your critical areas, critical times, vulnerabilities, and attackers' avenues of approach is what determines whether you are looking at your surroundings as an attacker or a defender. It's the same target, but your perception of those surroundings from an attacker's eyes should reflect real defenses, and the only way that is possible is if you see the perception the attacker is seeing, not the perception you are trying to present.

Perhaps you may remember the comic strip called *The Far Side*, written and illustrated by Gary Larson? In one of Larson's cartoons, four things were pictured: a rattlesnake, a spiky puffer fish, a domestic cat with its tail in the air and ears pinned back, and lastly, a man wearing a trench coat, with a shoe on his head, a swim floaty around his waist, and a bazooka in his left arm. The caption reads: "How nature says, 'Do not touch.'" Although comical, Larson pointed out a particular characteristic about attackers—many of their actions are animalistic, and when preparing to attack, they take on a mindset of internal commitment and aggression that allows them to effectively slow down time and space, while discarding morals and ethics, and focus on the biggest bang for their buck.

This change in demeanor, as Larson showed, displays characteristics that can be identified by individuals knowledgeable in specific behavior and characteristic of dangerous species. If you don't know what a puffer fish looks like when it is angry or threatened, you might think it was showing off or perhaps just a funny-looking fish. However, like most animals, the puffer fish will display certain characteristics (like puffing up) in an instinctual warning that something is about to happen. The same predictable characteristics Larson displayed in the cartoon strip are also true, and although a human attacker may not wear a floaty or a shoe on their head, they too will display certain characteristics when performing surveillance as well as when their attack is imminent.

Similar to animals that attack, human attackers don't typically feel bad for their targets, and in fact, they usually feel justified in their minds, seeing what they are doing as either okay as long as they don't get caught, or it's okay because it is for the greater good of their ideological belief or mood at the time of attack. Attacking another human being is the closest a person can get to exiting the human existence and stepping into the animalistic world, where life is based on survival of the fittest.

As you build a target package on what is important to you, do not concern yourself with morals and ethics or your religious barriers that typically hold you back from such thinking. This will only hinder you and your effectiveness at seeing weaknesses in your surroundings—weaknesses that possess the greatest draw for an attacker.

For the purpose of this book and what you will learn throughout, consider these two categories of the attacker's mindset and the coinciding phases of attack process that they represent; Attack Planner and Imminent Attacker. Individuals involved in both of these areas of planning and mindset will display their own unique behaviors, which should be understood by those defending against an attack, as they are reliable predictors of what stage the attack has reached.

When an individual in the attack-planning stage is carrying out on-scene foot or vehicle surveillance (Chapter 5), they are in their most vulnerable position because they are attempting to discover what they do not know, or they are trying to confirm what they perceive to be areas of vulnerability they can exploit.

This dance between an attack planner attempting to discover vulnerabilities to exploit and the defender trying to locate the attacker before they strike is the same dance performed daily by animals in the wild. Unfortunately for the human defender, cultures and societal allusions have crippled the natural tendency of people to instinctually seek clues to danger. Nothing is more beneficial for an attacker than this social evolution of self-imposed vulnerability.

Yet when an attacker is in the imminent phase of the attack, their behavior becomes even more predictable, especially if they are on a suicide mission. Predictability, however, does not mean the attacker will be any more identifiable to a person that walks blindly through life. A defender must ask themselves the basic questions of who, why, where, when, and how an attack could be carried out before being able to understand these predictable behaviors. For the individual being targeted, understanding these behavior characteristics could be the difference between life and death when an attack is imminent. Like the picture displayed by Larson, the imminent attackers' behaviors are nature's inescapable clue that danger is upon you.

Killing

Consciously killing is a very dark part of the human mind, and is perhaps the darkest area of any species' brain. Despite what scientists may theorize, humans are the only creatures on the face of the planet that murder for reasons other than instinctual survival. While it has been shown that many animals commit surplus killing for no other reason than to kill, their motivation will always have a sense of purity, as everything animals do in the wild is bound by their instinctual programming. When a new male lion takes over a pride, they often kill the young in order to repopulate with their own bloodline. Wolves may kill to eat and then keep killing in a frenzy brought on by blood lust or as a display of dominance. Whatever the reasons, the human species consciously kills knowing the significance of life and death. They consciously kill for reasons not bound to instinctual behavior. No other animal murders just because they consciously decided to do so. That is why humans will always be the alpha predator on the face of the earth, because we consciously, beyond instinct, kill.

Killing is an accepted part of warfare, and the justification for that killing will depend on whether you are in an offensive or defensive posture. Perhaps a military unit kills because they are threatened and therefore are displaying a defensive mechanism to protect their assets. With that threat comes an offensive, hostile movement by a separate leader or entity that may be trying to kill the opposition for dominance in a disputed area, as retaliation for a previous attack, or because their ideology is on the move and they are using force as a way to conquer. Terrorism is often rooted in an offensive killing mindset in the hope it will cause the outcome needed to bring a political change and allow a specific ideology to flourish. Mass killings, on the other hand, can actually be completely projected from a defensive mindset brought on by delusions and paranoia.

Regardless of the motivation behind the killing, successful attackers will most often approach the task with a similar mindset of target selection and attack-planning that is void of the consciousness the average human has on a daily basis. That is the mindset you are up against when developing true defenses and therefore you must entertain that approach when building your own target package.

Serial killers are perhaps the best examples of non-instinctual human killers. When I was in the FBI Academy, we received a brief from the behavioral science unit about serial killers. Their ability to coexist in a society while meticulously carrying out some of the most grotesque and barbaric killings in history was fascinating to some extent. These predators' decision-making process far surpasses the choice to kill, and in fact they systematically target specific individuals while taunting authorities. To say they do not have a conscience is a good description of their psyche. However, they do have a structured way of thinking that approaches methodical in their planning.

Serial killers are some of the most meticulous planners as well. Many of the targeting lessons you will learn in this book are used by predators like this, as well as the most deranged and violent criminals. It is a realistic statement to say these human predators are better at understanding individual vulnerabilities than most sane people will ever attempt to know.

However, serial killers are in fact suffering from psychological disorders and by and large have no ideological basis for their killing other than ego and sexual fulfillment. I would never categorize them as animalistic, because as I discussed earlier, I do not believe animals veer off the instinctual track when they kill. It is an insult to animals to place them on this, the lowest of levels in existence.

What I classify as the most dangerous killers are the ideological killers. Serial killers target specific people and mass killers pick a time and kill as many people as possible. But ideological killers systematically justify their actions on a conscious level and more often than not, will continue to kill as long as their ideology calls for those violent actions. As we have seen with the spread of fundamental Islamic jihad, millions of innocent individuals have been killed around the world in ways that are just as barbaric as the serial killers and mass murderers. The difference being that the jihadist knows full well what they are doing and in fact they are justifying it as the right thing to do. Terrorism, which is a tactic commonly used by jihadists, relies on this twisted marriage of so-called morals and killing for several reasons. First and foremost, it is used to recruit more and more ideological followers into action. Secondly, bloodthirsty killers, such as fundamental Islamic jihadists, use terrorism to place fear into the minds of civilians around the world, by demonstrating they intend to keep killing.

Do I expect you to embrace the minds of these killers? No, but I do want you to realize that attackers utilize techniques of information collection and targeting that we are all capable of doing, except you will ultimately be doing this targeting on yourself, family, business, city, etc. to gain awareness, build better defenses, and avoid attacks altogether. Now that you understand the reality of who will want to attack you and how you can use their tactics against them, lets look at the reality of what actually constitutes an attack.

CHAPTER 2

What Is an Attack?

AN ATTACK IS DEFINED as an aggressive and violent action against a person or thing. An attack is also typically the end result of information collected by an attacker into a target package in furtherance of an attack plan.

Remember this: the more an attacker can discover about your weaknesses, the more specific and detailed the attack will be. Likewise, the more you can discover about yourself, the greater your defenses will be and the less likely a successful attack can be carried out against you.

Most planned attacks are made up of a combination of information that you can actually collect yourself. Who would attack you? Why would they attack? Where would they attack? When would this attack be carried out? What type of attack would it most likely be? Finding the answers to these questions is the goal of this book. They are not impossible questions to answer, yet they are exactly what you need to consider in order to develop true awareness while gaining understanding of what kinds of attacks you could be caught up in.

Types of Attacks

The media, as well as many "experts" in the field of security, like to define attacks according to the individual or group that carries out the attack, the type of weapon used, or even the methodology employed. In the professional field of targeting, however, the type of attack is most often defined by the target's critical assets, critical areas, critical times, vulnerabilities that can be exploited and an attackers avenues of approach.

Any individual or group that attacks will follow this type of thought process. Regardless if the attacker is a basic street criminal, highly detailed serial killer, deranged mass murderer, homegrown terrorist operative, or terrorist group, certain discovery must be made about the target they wish to attack in order to gain effective results.

How many reports have you heard about a deranged mass murderer who aggressively shot up a fast-food restaurant at 3:00 a.m. on a Sunday? Basically none! That's because the discovery process of even a deranged attacker tells them that maximum casualties will be specific to certain locations and times. This is a harsh reality, but it's not a secret and in many cases is closer to subconscious knowledge than actual conscious discovery. However, as I will repeat again and again, the more you understand the end result of discovery by attackers, the greater your defenses will be against their attacks.

Now you see why the first step in understanding how to defend yourself and those around you is to define what exactly an attack is and how it is broken down into planning stages.

Understanding these pieces of the attack puzzle will help you develop better awareness and in turn help you plan and create better defenses.

In order to develop this understanding of what an attack actually is, it is important to look at the different types of attacks and identify which ones you should concentrate on for the purpose of this book.

Military Attacks

For the purpose of efficiency and clarity, this book will follow military-style attack-planning as closely as possible because military target packages are for the most part all-encompassing in their intelligence-collection on an enemy. Military attacks such as those carried out by Navy SEALs are effective because of two specific things: training and information collection. So let's take a closer look at how the SEALs go about it.

U.S. Navy SEALs take great effort to ensure the mission plan includes a detailed target package. Long before the mission is successfully carried out, these target packages are created using any target information (knowledge) available, which will give the SEALs a clear understanding of where, when, and how to attack a particular target. When this knowledge and understanding are combined with the years of effective and detailed training each SEAL must undergo, you get a perfect picture of the perfect attacking machine.

Make no mistake about it: SEALs are an offensive direct-action (attacker) force. They don't build schools or make nice with the local villagers—they attack. Although these attacks may include kidnapping a bad guy or destroying the infrastructure of a city, killing is and always will be the one thing they do better and more efficiently than any other military unit in the world, and it all starts by developing a detailed target package on the enemy they are offensively targeting.

04:45 a.m. At a barren compound in eastern Afghanistan, the darkness is penetrated by the sudden deafening noise from U.S. Army Blackhawk helicopters from the legendary 160th Special Operations Aviation Regiment (SOAR), better known as the "Night Stalkers." On board the helicopters is a task force of U.S. military special forces operators comprised of U.S. Navy SEALs, U.S. Air Force Combat Controllers (CCT), U.S. Navy Explosive Ordinance Disposal (EOD) operators, and combat-hardened military working dogs. As three aircrafts touch down outside the compound walls, another hovers about fifteen feet above the roof of the center compound building. The operators fast-rope from the fourth helicopter and secure the roof, then take up overwatch positions as the operators from the helicopters outside the compound move toward the main gate and swiftly breach the doors. While all the operators moved into and around the target, the helicopters lifted off and moved to a predetermined area to loiter away from the target just far enough away that they could quickly return to pick up the operators. This procedure was imperative because of the heightened potential for Rocket-Propelled Grenades (RPG) to bring down a helicopter in the vicinity of the target.

Now inside the compound, the operators move quickly, clearing multiple small huts, then moving toward the main building in the center of the compound where the SEALs on the rooftop have already started clearing from the roof downward. As the task-force operators make entry into the bottom floor of the main building and clear the first level, the SEALs that have been moving downward from the roof make contact with and secure the target on the second floor. Calling out over the radio to inform the task force and the commanders located at the Tactical Operations Command, seventy-five miles away, that the target has been secured, the task force moves toward the gates they had previously breached in preparation to call the helicopters in for an extraction.

After initial contact with the helicopters for an extraction, half of the task force re-clears the immediate area outside the compound's main gate as the rest of the operators follow close behind and move to an adjacent field approximately 100-yards away. The task-force operators spread out and crouch down into a long perimeter that is split into four different groups separated far enough apart from each other that each helicopter can land next to a group. Amazingly, within two minutes of calling for the extraction, the helicopters seemingly appeared out of nowhere, slamming down so close to the operators that they literally stand up, take two steps, and they are inside the birds. Within sixty seconds, all personnel are loaded onto the helicopters and a full headcount is affirmed. Just as quickly as they had arrived, the Night Stalkers disappeared into the darkness as the sound of their rotors fade into the night wind.

Time on target = less than 10 minutes. Mission accomplished!

How is it possible for so many moving parts to come together in such an effective manner? And what does this realistic fictional story have to do with average civilians wanting to be safer in their own life? In order to carry out a proper attack as complex as the one described above, all variables must be considered, and all possible vulnerabilities must be mitigated. This is achieved by building a proper target package that will help the

SEALs and everyone else involved understand where the critical areas are located, the critical times for those areas, and how to exploit the vulnerabilities in and around the compound.

Criminal Attacks

Criminal attacks come in many forms and typically involve motivations of personal gain for the attacker. In the interest of simplicity, I have categorized criminal attacks into four main motivational categories: material, monetary, emotion, and ego-driven attacks.

Robbery and burglary most likely occur for material and/or monetary gain, while things like revenge, sexual deviation, kidnapping, rape, serial killing, gang violence, and manslaughter (due to road rage, etc.) can be categorized as emotional or ego-driven motivations.

Emotional and ego-driven attacks are often planned, but they can also be impulsive due to conflicts such as domestic issues, workplace pressures, or bar fights. Material and monetary attacks, on the other hand, typically follow a known plan or system of TTPs. The more elaborate the crime, the more in-depth the attack planning becomes, but in almost all cases, the target is a specific individual person or thing, or a cross section of people or things.

Terrorist Attacks

Terrorism is likely the most familiar term in this book. Interestingly, however, most people do not actually know the definition of terrorism. They see a bombing by a certain group and think it's automatically terrorism and the people who committed the bombing are automatically terrorists. But this isn't exactly true, because terrorism is not a group or any specific type of attack; it is a *tactic*. Terrorism is the use of fear, intimidation, and violence for a political aim. Why is this important for you to realize? Because it helps you understand why certain targets would be picked, and why certain areas are more inviting to individuals that carry out attacks to achieve a political gain.

In the past, individuals and groups that committed terrorist acts were focused on grand attacks that caused widespread damage and large numbers of fatalities. In recent history however, this focus has changed and, as predicted by myself and others in the field of targeting analysis, a shift toward smaller, more frequent and bloody attacks has occurred. This shift has happened for several reasons, including the fact that grand-style attacks require greater manpower, financing, and more in-depth mission-planning, which is not the case in smaller, less sophisticated attacks that utilize knives and guns and easily accessed populated areas. Also, focus has changed to incorporate more residential locations where the average person goes to relax or do their business. Malls, restaurants, entertainment venues, places of worship, and educational locations have become targets, because the attackers have realized you do not have to have a grand attack to put fear into a large section of the population when you have social media as your magnifier. You just have to hit them where they're comfortable and then broadcast it to the world.

It's also important for you to understand that the motivation for attackers to pick certain targets can shift, and it can suddenly encompass locations you may have deemed safe in the past. So as you continue to read this book, remember: when you contemplate the attacker mindset, you must understand the who and why just as much as the when, where, and how.

History has shown what we call *terrorism* to actually be one of the oldest subversive tactics known to man, and in modern terms it is best defined as unconventional warfare. In many cases, it is the only way for a small organization or ideology to effectively change the strategic outcome of a conflict. Changing the name of this tactic throughout history has made it more palatable, but the characteristics are always similar: using unconventional tactics, improvised devices, and small units to attack, more often than not, civilian targets.

Unconventional warfare is a tactical way of fighting that makes pinpoint strikes instead of grand takeovers of territory and, concentrates efforts to affect the psyche of the enemy's population or government. The attacks are well thought out and made to have an impact on the strategic big picture.

Sometimes, as in the 2004 bombing attacks on the commuter train system in Madrid, Spain, a terrorist attack can actually affect the outcome of political elections. Although this is rare, the Madrid train bombings did just that. The attacks were nearly simultaneous, coordinated bombings carried out three days before Spain's general elections on the morning of March 11, 2004. 192 people died and 1,800 were wounded. Although no particular group's participation was established, the official investigation indicated the attacks were directed by an al-Qaeda–inspired terrorist cell. These attacks are a good example of an attack planner picking the best area, time, and avenues of approach to carry out a mass casualty hit.

As history shows, all sectors of our daily lives have been attacked at some point. In each of these examples of successful attacks by terrorists, target packages were completed and specific attacks were chosen to effectively and efficiently get the "biggest bang for the buck."

Random Violence

Yes, there are such things as random acts of violence, where a person is victimized simply for being in the wrong place at the wrong time. However even random acts are typically carried out in areas that lend themselves to one important fact: people are located there. Whether it's at midnight on a lonely sidewalk or in the middle of a crowded New York City park, if there were no people present to victimize, the random act of violence would most likely be an act of vandalism or something like animal cruelty.

Always remember that mentally unstable individuals are a part of life in any culture, and some of them can be perpetrators of random acts of violence. When you add to that the increased use of drugs that is running rampant, not only in our country but around the world, you also have an increased threat of possible attacks by deranged individuals.

Instigated Attacks

Have you ever been to a bar where a fight broke out? Have you attended a Little League game where parents, angry about a referee's call, got into arguments and ended up committing violence against one another? Have you ever been involved with or seen a road rage incident that led to a violent altercation? These are all examples of attacks that are spur of the moment and in many cases instigated by two or more parties.

I will simply say this about these types of attacks: They are 100-percent avoidable. If you're an adult, unless you are physically being assaulted or somebody is in imminent danger, just walk or drive away, depending on the situation.

If you do find yourself in a bad situation that you may have started because of your anger or because you were too prideful to let it go, take my advice: Swallow your anger or pride and look for a quick exit. By and large this has nothing to do with the tactics found in this book, but the law-enforcement officer in me feels it is important to remind you that fights you choose to get involved with, that could be avoided, often end up in hospital time at best and jail time at worst. And in some cases, long jail sentences because a single punch can cause serious bodily harm or even a fatality. Even if you were somehow "in the right," you're still looking at years of legal costs and untold stress that you could have avoided altogether if you had just walked away.

PART 2

BUILDING AN ATTACKER'S TARGET PACKAGE

In the first section, we performed a deep dive covering what the attacker's mindset actually is, in order to help you understand how an attacker contemplates an attack, and how they will build an attack package as the initial step in the overall attack plan. With that detailed overview, your understanding of the initial steps for building a target package should be solid and you should already start to see how compiling this information can be beneficial in building better defenses, increasing awareness, and in most circumstances, avoiding attacks altogether. When a defender realizes that aggressive, accurate attackers have developed the same knowledge as they have on a target's critical areas, critical times, vulnerabilities, and attackers' avenues of approach, the defender should be able to reverse their own knowledge and apply it from an attacker's point of view by simply changing their mindset back and forth from attacker to defender mode.

Let's discuss how you can collect information on targets from an attacker's point of view. We will concentrate on two main areas of collection: remote information collection (via computer) and ground surveillance (on scene of the actual location of attack).

Also, we will be focusing on the Target Equation that you can use to simplify your information collection. Based on the understanding you have developed up to this point, you can see that defining an attack by who carries it out or the weapon/method being employed is secondary to the development of a target package in the overall attack plan. At its most simplistic level, an attack can be defined as the specific discoveries included in a target package of a chosen target. This includes the specific categories of a target's critical assets (CA), critical areas (CAR), critical times (CT), its vulnerabilities (V), attackers' avenues of approach (AVP), combined with effective tactics (TAC), techniques (TQS), and procedures (P), and motivation (M) of the specific attackers themselves. Remember, this equation is not meant to completely mimic law-enforcement and military target packages, but it will encompass all the information you will need to complete a target package on yourself and your surroundings:

$$(CA+CAR+CT+V+AVP) + (TAC+TQS+P+M) = \text{Target Equation}$$

CHAPTER 3

Charting Target
Package Information

ASSEMBLING A TARGET PACKAGE is the first step an attacker will take in preparation for an attack, long before weapons are acquired, financing is secured, or a mission plan is finalized. It is how an attacker defines why a specific target will be chosen, what is needed to carry out an attack on that target, and the best direction and time to hit the target. Developing a target package constitutes a series of steps taken to develop an overall understanding of what makes a viable target. By developing a target package on yourself, it will allow you, the defender, to understand when, where, and how you could end up in the middle of an attack. Just as important, it will help you identify the safest areas and times to go about your daily life, and instill an understanding of how to realistically prepare and respond to possible incidents.

The motivation behind specific target selection often depends on what an individual or group wants to gain from the attack. Knowing this helps you realistically understand how each part of your life could be attacked and who would carry out the attack, as well as give you an educated prediction of the probability of an attack. Remember, attack probability and attack possibility are two different things. Your workplace or school may not have a high attack probability for a deranged attacker compared to other locations when defined by statistical analysis, but the possibility of an attack is still 100-percent, as is proven every time a workplace or school attack is carried out. Unless you are psychic and can tell the future, or you have credible sources on the street, you will never know exactly which location is in imminent danger. Therefore, you must assume an attack on any location is possible.

Anyone building a target package wants to know as much information as they can find about the target. Once they have that information, they want to figure out where their target's weaknesses and vulnerabilities lie. Attackers often look for certain "indicators" that clarify whether a target that claims to be hardened actually is, and if the population is aware of their surroundings. For instance, a military-style target package will consist of any amount of information (intelligence) that can be collected on a target. This information includes things like history of the target, size and effectiveness of enemy forces, local terrain, uniforms or lack thereof, religious beliefs, number of battle-tested forces, communications equipment, vehicle and foot patrols, and so on.

How this information is collected will be discussed in detail later. However, as you proceed in gaining an understanding of a target package, you must continuously focus your mindset toward an attacker's perspective that we discussed in Chapter 1, which will give you a better understanding for what you need to collect and how it is collected in order to form an accurate attack package of yourself. For now, you should start to concentrate on a few terms as they will continuously be repeated over and over throughout the book so that everywhere you look, you will be able to identify what attackers are seeking.

Critical Assets are the very things that if removed from a location, would cause the target to cease functioning or to have a reduction in capacity to function. Air conditioning is a huge critical asset to tall buildings and entertainment facilities. If the A/C goes out in these facilities, the patrons will stop going there, the workers will revolt and computers could stop working properly. So for the purpose of disrupting a facility, destroying the A/C in summer would be an effective attack on a critical asset. For the purpose of this book, you are considered a critical asset, so it is a term we will just assume is being referred to as we talk about your own target package, however when thinking with the attacker's mindset you should be looking at all the critical assets of places that you could be attacked or be caught up in an attack.

The areas where those A/Cs are located would be considered a Critical Area, as it is the area where an attacker that wanted to carry out this particular type of disruptive attack would target. This critical area is also where the majority of surveillance by mission planners would be focused so that is an area critical for them as well because if they are caught testing the security in that area, it could result in the more robust defenses by the target and more importantly, cancellation of the mission itself.

Most targets have set times for when they are most vulnerable. People, buildings, and even whole cities have the Critical Times where mission planners and attackers will be able to access their intended targets much easier inside the critical areas. In the case of a facility's A/C, remote information could be collected on a critical asset and its critical area via a computer search for all possible information. Schedules, satellite imagery, social norms etc., all can be collected via the Internet for many targets (including your life). Security could then be tested through on-scene surveillance in a vehicle and even on foot, during working hours and during non-working hours to see if facility workers are more alert during busy times or during slow hours. Remember the closer a mission planner gets to the target during surveillance, the more dangerous it is for them and the easier it is for the defender to pick up on their nonverbal signals that they are up to no good. Once the mission planner determines when security is most relaxed, they have effectively discovered that targets critical time.

While the mission planners are performing remote and on scene surveillance, they will make notes of other vulnerabilities that could be exploited. Do people dress a certain way? Are there specific uniforms at that facility? Do they lack sophisticated card readers? These are all considered exploitable vulnerabilities that a mission planner could list in a target package and an attacker could use to their benefit.

The last part of your specific points of focus for a target package will be Avenues of Approach. When mission planners are developing all their knowledge through information collection and on-scene tests, they will be taking notes on which way the attacker should approach the target. This is often determined by the other criteria we discussed already, as well as what type of attack is going to be carried out. Are the attackers able to run the A/C systems over with a truck at night? That avenue of approach would be completely different from an A/C system that was placed on top of a tall building only accessible through an unsecured rooftop door. Each target will have its own specific critical assets, critical areas, critical times, vulnerabilities, and attackers' avenues of approach. That is what the mission planners want to discover and what the attackers will use, and it is what you will want to know in order to outthink them and increase your awareness and possibility of avoiding attacks altogether.

When building a target package on yourself and your surroundings, utilizing the attacker's mindset, it is important to focus on all aspects of the target far beyond visual defenses. For instance, a lack of awareness (also known as complacency) is one of the most common indicators an attacker can discover and later exploit. This "unawareness" can be found almost anywhere, from your long-time city-dwelling citizen to a seasoned law-enforcement officer. No matter their background, anyone living in and around a certain routine or culture can develop unhealthy habits of complacency, this specific information would be a part of a target package. For example, the first and most common lapse in awareness by professionals and civilians alike is in thinking there's a greater possibility of a specific person, place, or event being attacked if there is a "known threat" or a raised "threat level" even when it is based on accurate intelligence. In other words, just because there is a heightened threat level or known threat against a person, place, or event doesn't mean the possibility of attack is absolutely higher than a low-threat area, or that forewarned locations or people will be adequately prepared.

Every sector, private and public schools, stadiums, convention centers, theaters, arenas, work locations, restaurants, places of worship, airports, shopping malls, hotels and resorts, along with every sex, age, race, and belief—all have been attacked, often unexpectedly. Therefore, an attack can happen anywhere and at any time, and in most cases, it happens with no known threat or heightened attack threat level. Whether by a petty criminal or a war-hardened terrorist, a deranged attacker or sex offender, every sector of your daily life has seen its own threat at one time or another. Now, does this mean that any of this will ever happen to you? The odds actually say no, and that we all are more likely to fall victim to a car crash or illness at some point. I know this sounds like doom and gloom, but it is actually better to be aware of these statistics than to live in oblivion and possibly put yourself in the wrong place at the wrong time as a result.

Having spent many years in government service observing and operating in an environment that dealt with planning attacks, attempting to figure out who, why, where, when, and how an attack may happen, I was forced to see the reality of possibilities relating to potential attacks. As I transitioned from naïve Navy officer candidate recruit to a well-trained operator and later a seasoned investigator, I realized that paranoia is something that individuals uneducated in the benefits of being aware tend to subscribe to, and awareness is a state of mind that most people avoid. I began to take mental notes of the daily threats that surrounded me in every aspect of my own life and utilize the targeting methodology that I was responsible for in my professional career. I would flip the switch from attacker to defender to see how my routines could be altered to mitigate various threats. I was for the first time building a target package on every aspect of my life.

For example, in my job as an FBI Special Agent in New York, I was tasked with targeting areas to discover the most likely areas that an attack could occur. I always approached this part of my job not from the defender's perspective, but from an attacker's viewpoint utilizing my unconventional warfare training I received as a SEAL. I went even further in my targeting to the point where I would spend weeks identifying as an attacker from the time I woke up until I went to bed. Vulnerabilities began to pop up everywhere around me on individual and citywide levels. I noticed when people approached a busy intersection, they would quite often not look up from their phone. As I began to pay closer attention to this, I noticed it wasn't just intersections. I saw people walking drunk late at night while they texted, or getting on a train at the Freedom Tower in lower Manhattan, where the 9/11 attacks happened. Never once did any of these people look up to see if anything unusual was happening. Unbeknownst to them, they had inadvertently increased the probability of an attack happening to them, or not being able to react if something happened close by. Lucky for them, as I watched them, contemplating attacks, I was still the good guy.

I want you to read this next story with an attacker's mindset and see if you can start to envision the critical areas and critical times along with the vulnerabilities that could be exploited and where you, as an attacker, would make your approach. Then, as you continue through the scenarios in this book, you should find yourself more understanding of how the attackers were able to pinpoint the same criticalities and include them in their attack packages before they carried out their attacks.

One warm spring night in New York City, I was leaving a bar on the Lower East Side of Manhattan at about 2:30 a.m. with a friend of mine that was an agent from another agency. As we turned the corner onto a quiet street, we saw a female so drunk she could barely walk. My buddy and I both knew what we should do, so we followed her from a distance to make sure she got home without being assaulted. What we thought would be a few blocks of anonymous good Samaritan protection of a fellow New Yorker turned out to be a 45-minute stroll across midtown.

As the young woman walked, we monitored other individuals that passed her by. Many of the passersby were laughing, while a few guys literally stopped and schemed to approach her. Instead, my buddy and I approached them, quickly identified ourselves and told them to keep on moving. Finally, as the young woman walked into her building she was greeted by her doorman before disappearing into the elevator. She never knew she had two federal agent bodyguards that escorted her home.

Unfortunately, that level of protection is not typical for most intoxicated people walking home late at night, and I kept thinking the entire time, this woman has no idea how vulnerable she is, at such a critical area at a critical time. She was a sitting duck and the attacker's avenue of approach was literally from any direction. When I got home, I reviewed that entire event from the defender's point of view and it was quite apparent that if most people simply understood how attackers thought and planned attacks by building a target package, and if they could realize how they could apply this knowledge in their own daily lives, they would probably never put themselves in this type of vulnerable dilemma.

Consequently, I realized I was guilty myself of major complacency in many aspects of my life such as paying too much attention to my phone and not my surroundings as I walked through my daily life. Most likely I would have fallen victim to complacency had I not started to formulate this attack package on myself. Think about that and let it sink in. I'm a trained warrior, serving as an FBI agent in a city that is known as the biggest bullseye for terrorists in the world, and I was comfortably complacent. Imagine the rabbit hole that most civilians live in on a daily basis and you will realize how vulnerable most people are (maybe you) on a daily basis.

So, having woken myself back up, I changed my habits. By simply taking my eyes off my phone at predetermined areas that could be an issue, like crossing the road, or when I was walking out of the federal building on the way to my car, I increased my awareness level tremendously. Expanding on this quest to understand how, or if, it was possible to wake up an entire population and empower them with awareness, I sought out and talked to several people I knew from Israel, mainly because the Israeli population is a great example of a citizenry that lives under a constant threat yet is able to maintain heightened awareness without subscribing to paranoia. What I discovered is that the citizens of Israel are able to stay safe and sane because they understand who their enemy is and the history of their attacks, and it's as if they all have their own little target packages floating around in their minds. This, in turn, allows them to effectively see where the biggest vulnerabilities exist to the critical areas and critical times in their lives. In fact, many Israelis have avoided becoming a casualty because of their heightened awareness, which is rooted in an understanding of the mindset of those that want to do them harm.

In contrast to the Israeli civilians self-defense posture, building target packages on enemies of the United States is the job left to our military as well as various intelligence and law-enforcement agencies. Similarly as you saw in the previous chapters, criminals, terrorists, serial killers, child predators, and other individuals or groups wanting to attack you will also build target packages in an effort to try to discover and chart your critical areas, your critical times, and the vulnerabilities they can exploit in order to carry out an effective attack. In other words, you know your life better than most attackers, and in order to be successful at attacking you, the bad guy must learn what you know and exploit it. So, as you read the case studies throughout this book, you should be considering how the attackers utilized the common aspects of daily life in and around a target in order to build their target packages.

Every incident in the case studies we will cover that involves a victim and an attack started with the attackers formulating a target package that utilized information about the targets' critical areas, critical times, vulnerabilities, and the attackers' avenues of approach. And in each attack, their target packages allowed the attackers to forward-think and outmaneuver the defending authorities. Likewise, every case study that demonstrates successful forward thinking and defensive posture also started out with a well-thought-out target package. In order to attack, they have to understand you, and in order to defend yourself, you have to understand the attacker. It's that deadly dance we discussed earlier with the animals in the wild, and it revolves around a dance floor known as an attack package.

As I said at the beginning of this chapter, assembling a target package is the first step an attacker will take in preparation for an attack, because it is the process of discovering information on a target that individuals wishing to attack will need to penetrate defenses and figure out the direction and scope of their attack. So, let's move to the next step and put this new mindset and understanding to work by demonstrating how you should chart your target package information, followed by how you collect and verify these specific details. Let's build an attack package!

Populating the Target Equation

It is important for you not to get overwhelmed by the thought of building a target package as you will not need the same level of detail in your target packages as military or law-enforcement targeting experts, as their in-depth studies include mission specific goals of catching, killing, or prosecuting bad guys. Your target packages will focus on awareness, avoidance, and actions you can take if you are ever caught up in a violent situation.

When I was in college, I worked as a fitness instructor, and I could always tell who showed up to get into shape and who showed up to just be at the gym. The people who got the most out of my instruction were the people who listened to what I was saying and then built upon that instruction with an emphasis on changing their lifestyles. Rather than lay every ounce of targeting information for you to just carry around, I am trying to convince you to engage your mind by fully targeting yourself. Now there are other books in this genre that try to give you everything you need. But the way I see it, and the way I teach it, is that in order for me to fully increase your awareness, I need to give you insight into the attacker's mindset and what an attack is, and I have. However, that does little to prepare you to take action if you are ever caught up in an attack. Your brain must be fully prepared before that day comes, so your actions after you read this book are just as important as the actual process of understanding what's inside it.

Remote information collection is the first step in collecting specific target planning information that you will input into the target package equation, followed by on-site collection that takes you closer to the target so you can actually see the size and scope of attacks that could happen as predicted in the target equation. Remember there are two parts to this equation:

1. Information concerning your criticalities and vulnerabilities (**CA+CAR+CT+V+ AVP**).
2. Information (mostly historical) concerning your enemy's tactics, techniques and procedures (**TAC+TQS+P+M**).

After you collect that information and lay it out in an organized fashion, you will be able to make sense of what you are looking at when you perform on-site surveillance.

Step 1: Divide Your Life Into Sectors

Finally, you will now see exactly how these criticalities apply to your life, and how they help dissect the different areas of your daily life called sectors. To determine your different sectors, you should first divide your daily life into as many parts as possible, which will make it much easier to organize the criticalities you face throughout the day. Start with the time you wake up and, step-by-step, separate each part of the day into sectors and label them with a word that defines them.

Sectors

- Home
- Work
- School
- Restaurant/bar
- Stadiums and arenas
- Outdoor special events
- Places of worship
- Bank
- Airport
- Field trips

Step 2: Dissect Sectors Into Critical Assets, Critical Areas, and Critical Times

The next step is splitting these sectors into the first three criticalities (critical assets, critical areas, and critical times) in order to break them down into more specific areas of concentration. The last two criticalities (vulnerabilities and attackers' avenues of approach) will follow in STEP 3 and STEP 4.

Let's go deeper into the details of the first and most familiar sector (Home) by dissecting it into the first three criticalities.

Sector

- HOME
  - *Critical Assets*
  - *Critical Areas*
  - *Critical Times*

Now dissect those criticalities into as many detailed bullet points as it takes to fully display a complete picture of the sector (Home) that an attacker would need to plan an attack. Try to pull up this information from your memory and from the computer using search techniques that will be discussed in Chapter 4:

Remote Surveillance. Starting below, you will see how the detail of these criticalities gets more and more attack-specific as we dissect them further and further.

Sector

- **HOME**
  - *Critical Assets*
  —**Family**
    - ° One wife
    - ° One husband
    - ° Kids
      - · Two young children
        - ~One boy (nine years old)
        - ~One girl (seven years old)
      - · One teenage girl (fourteen years old)
      - · One Australian sheep dog
  —**House**
    - ° Three-bedroom, ranch-style home with garage
  —**Car**
    - ° Chevy Tahoe
  —**Weapons**
    - ° Three hand guns
  —**Food**
  —**Water**
    - ° City water
  —**Electricity**
  —**Gas**
  —**Money**

—Keys
- *Critical Areas*
  —Yard
  o Back yard fenced in
  —Children's bedroom(s)
  —Adults' bedrooms
  —Doors
  —Windows
  —A/C unit
  —Garage
- *Critical Times*
  —8 a.m.–4 p.m.
  (everyone is gone; home is empty)
  —9 p.m.–5 a.m.
  (everyone is asleep)

Step 3: List Vulnerabilities for the First Three Criticalities

At this point you are starting to put a picture together by getting deeper in the target package. We then chose a sector to develop (for the sake of this exercise, that sector is "Home"), and now we can start pulling out specifics found by looking online for an even deeper dive to specify what could be exploited and who might exploit it. Although your home is what we are paying particular attention to now, you should still look online to see what you can find about yourself and your house, along with every other sector. This is because you need to see what attackers could find online and use for target analysis.

Sector

- ■ HOME
  - • *Critical Assets*
  - —Family
    - ○ One wife
    - ○ One husband
      - · Without the parents, family would suffer and possibly be split up from one another
      - · Parents have access to guns, cash, etc.
    - ○ Kids
      - · **Two young children**
        - ~**One boy (nine years old)**
        - ~**One girl (seven years old)**
          - -Very helpless as most young children are
          - -Prone to finding trouble and wandering off
          - -Can be easy prey for child predators
      - · **One teenaged girl (fourteen years old)**
        - -Extremely forgetful
        - -Main person responsible for leaving doors, windows, and garage unlocked or open
        - -Can be easy prey for sexual predators
    - ○ **One Australian sheep dog**
      - · Family dog is expensive
      - · Dog stays in the house during the day but has doggy door to back yard
      - · Neighbor's dog stolen and used as bait in dog fighting ring in nearby city

—House
- All family belongings are in the home
  · Three handguns (in a safe inside the garage)
  · Jewelry and emergency cash (in a safe inside the garage)
- Young kids' rooms located on the same side of the house as the A/C central-air system
- Young kids' rooms have large accessible windows outside the fenced-in area
- Typically empty during critical day times and while on vacation

—Car
- Necessity for transportation of family
- Important for recreational issues (i.e., Boy Scouts)
- Gets parents to work and home from work
- Emergency vehicle if someone needs to go to the hospital
- Used to run errands, pick up food, etc.
- Often left on empty
- Parked in driveway despite having a garage

—Weapons
- Three handguns (in a safe inside the garage)
- 300 rounds of 9mm ammunition (in a safe inside the garage)

—Food
- Food is bought week by week
- Not a lot of nonperishables
- Have a small garden in back yard but only small amounts of common vegetables available

—**Water**
  ○ Home connected to city water
  ○ No bottled water is stored in the home
  ○ No backup water source (i.e., water purifier)

—**Electricity**
  ○ Local electric company
  ○ Necessary for sustaining life at home
  ○ Central air A/C and heat are electric, located outside the privacy fence
  ○ No backup generator

—**Gas**
  ○ Stove is gas-operated
  ○ Propane tank for the grill outside by the storage shed in the back yard, inside the privacy fence

—**Money**
  ○ Reserve money kept in a garage safe
  ○ Both parents get paid every two weeks
  ○ Husband's check is direct deposit
  ○ Wife's check has to be hand-deposited

—**Keys**
  ○ Essential for locking and unlocking the front door
  ○ Essential for use of the car
  ○ Supposed to be stored next to front door on hanger
  ○ Usually lost in the house somewhere

• *Critical Areas*
—**Yard**
  ○ Front yard is not fenced in and allows access to children's bedroom window as well as central A/C and heat unit

- ° Back yard is fenced-in with high wooden privacy fence
- **—Children's bedroom(s)**
  - ° Located towards front of house unprotected by privacy fence
- **—Adults' bedrooms**
  - ° In the back of the house, protected by the privacy fence
- **—Doors**
  - ° **Wooden front door**
    - · Often left unlocked by children and teenager
  - ° **Back sliding doors**
    - · Often left unlocked by children and teenager
  - ° **Entryway also through the garage**
    - · Often left unlocked by children and teenager
- **—Windows**
  - ° Located in every room in the house
  - ° Often open in spring and fall
  - ° Often left unlocked by teenager and children
- **—A/C unit**
  - ° Located outside privacy fence, directly below children's room window
- **—Garage**
  - ° **Large gun safe**
    - · Three pistols
    - · 300 rounds of ammunition
    - · Family reserve cash
  - ° **Garage door often left up by accident**

- *Critical Times*
  —8 a.m.–4 p.m. (everyone is gone; home is empty)
  - ○ Statistically most likely time for burglary
  —9 p.m.–5 a.m. (everyone is asleep)
  - ○ Statistically most likely time for robbery and child abduction

Step Four: Identify the Attackers' Avenues of Approach

—**Freeway**
  - ○ Easy access to the neighborhood
  - ○ Quick getaway

—**Creek located outside rear privacy fence**
  - ○ Easy place for criminals to covertly access neighborhood

—**Several windows and doors around the house**
  - ○ Open windows and doors create easy access to house for nefarious individuals

These lists are not exhaustive, but they are a good example of how easy this process is to take the attacker's mindset and dissect your life and all its sectors. As you will see in the last step of the attack equation, all of the information collected will be compiled into a predictive chart of who, why, where, when, and how an attack could happen in a specific sector.

Step Five: Completing the Target Equation

When you chart specifics concerning history and the tactics, techniques, and procedures of attackers you have narrowed down, make sure you fully understand which sector(s) that it relates to. You will find when you are considering most targets, you will already know what type of attacks could be carried out in and around the target areas because, as I keep saying over and over, you know your area far better than any outside source.

Now, when you combine the information collected for the first four previous steps of this target equation, you can clearly see that *Sector* **HOME** has specific types of attacks, times of attacks and vulnerabilities with high possibilities of being exploited. In other words, you have now identified who, why, where, when, and how the highest possibility of attack exists for the sector HOME.

Sector

- **HOME**
  - *Most Critical Areas*
    —Children's windows and area around the central A/C
    —Front and back doors
    —Garage
  - *Attackers' Avenues of Approach*
    —Nearby freeway allows for quick to and from the neighborhood
    —Deep, dry creek bed behind the house allows for stealthy access to the neighborhood
  - *The Sum of Sector HOME's Target Equation*
    —Type of Attack
    - ○ Time of attack
      - · Vulnerabilities
    —Robbery
    - ○ Evenings 9 p.m.–5 a.m.
      - · Family sleeping, doors, windows, garage unlocked, easy access for criminals into the neighborhood from the nearby freeway

—Burglary
  ◦ Daytime 8 a.m.–5 p.m.
    · No one is home, easy access for criminals into the neighborhood from the nearby freeway
—Child Abduction
  ◦ Evenings 5 p.m.–8 a.m. (following day)
    · Helpless children, outdoors a lot; windows are outside the privacy fence; windows unlocked; children's room on the opposite side of parents'
—Pedophile Infiltration into Family
  ◦ Infiltration covers a period of time needed for a pedophile to work their way into the family
    · Pedophile lives in the neighborhood, could befriend the family anywhere
—Burglary of Copper in the Central A/C
  ◦ Daytime 8 a.m.–5 p.m.
    · A/C unit located outside the privacy fence with easy access; unit camouflaged by thick brush
—Burglary/Robbery of Safe in Garage
  ◦ Burglary: Daytime 8 a.m.–5 p.m.; Robbery: Nighttime 5 p.m.–8 a.m.
    · Garage door often left open, safe is located close to the garage door, not the back wall, most likely criminals will only know it's a safe, but not what is actually inside
—Theft of Family Dog
  ◦ Daytime 8 a.m.–5 p.m.
    · Able to get out through back gate when left open; local dogs have been stolen for fighting dogs to train gang members' fighting dogs

—Burglary/Robbery of Family Car
  ○ Anytime car is parked in the driveway
    · Garage is so full that the family cars cannot be
    parked inside

Now you can see how easy it is to take what you know and combine it with the mindset of someone who would exploit that information for nefarious purposes. In this exercise we only concentrated on someone's home. However, it is possible to dissect any other sector of your life, business, schools, stadiums, city, and so on the same way.

Had this exercise been done by any of the patrons who were visiting special events over the past few years where simple but deadly terror attacks occurred, there is a good chance they would have been aware enough to either avoid the location where the attacks happened, or their actions in response to what was happening could have saved their lives because they would have been able to properly think their way to safety. Likewise, had local authorities and the private facility managers done the same type of exercise, they could have set up better observation to catch mission planners doing surveillance and/or develop better security measures based on their criticalities.

Basically, what has been missing from everyone else's equation is actual participation and proper guidance, instead everyone relies on (and pays) "experts" to protect them. But now you know that the things that are listed above are not only exploitable by an attacker, but they can also be mitigated and lessened by you very easily, because you now know more than the attackers and mission planners and you know where to look in order to spot them because you have charted exactly where they will be in an attempt to gain more and more information.

Chapter 4 will help you understand what general information you can collect, where you can collect it, and how attention to past and current historical trends will be the majority of information you will seek on attacker TTPs and general target information. Then, in Chapter 5, you will see how this information is verified on-site for more detailed analysis of the target.

Also, as you begin your own target package, make sure that you take into account individual day(s) criticalities as well as the fact that weekday schedules will be drastically different from weekends and nights will be completely different from days. Winter schedules will be different from summer and vacations will be different from when you are home in your daily grind. Take a few hours when nothing is on TV and it is rainy outside. Dissect your life into sectors and I guarantee if you have read to this point in the book, you will start to see the attack plans develop before you even chart them.

It doesn't have to be fancy or with graphics, you can simply take a pen and paper and jot down pertaining information as you search, just use the expanding format I have shown above to keep it neat and easily understandable and updatable. I actually find cutting and pasting things into a document I can share on my phone from my computer to be the best practice for people on the go and it's also easiest to share with family members when it is viewable on a cellphone.

CHAPTER 4

Remote Information Collection

Tools for Remote Surveillance

- Internet
- Mapping programs
- Library
- Newspapers

General Online Information Collection

General information is the easiest of all information to collect. When you go onto a computer to collect basic information about a target, it is possible to find out hours of operation, event times and dates, addresses, demographics, past incidents, and even shared threats. Most of us do this type of general information collection on a daily basis without even realizing it when we are seeking a place to eat, a movie to watch, or entering travel information into a GPS device. All of this is exactly the general information that attackers collect remotely when building an attack package.

Collecting information usually starts far away from the target and slowly works you inward without any fancy gadgets or training. Remember, most attackers would rather never set foot near a target location before an attack if possible, as this is the most vulnerable area and time for their attack to be thwarted. If an attacker is recognized or questioned when performing surveillance (this includes petty criminals and terrorists alike), they are less likely to actually carry out an attack at that location. Basically, if a target is too hardened or if the awareness is too great, the attacker will go elsewhere and pick a softer target, and so you should begin to understand why discovering as much as possible remotely is so important for building an attack package.

All City Layouts are Similar in an Attacker's Eyes

A perfect example of how remote information collection sets the foundation of the overall attack package is displayed in one of my own personal experiences that occurred shortly before I attended the FBI Academy in 2005. I was working on a citywide project to demonstrate how on-site verification helps an attacker see the breadth and scope of a target as well as possible hidden vulnerabilities. But, as with any target package, I did some thorough online research to begin my target package. Although I intended to emphasize the on-site verification of information, I began to discover how important remote information collection actually was and how our modern technology had actually eliminated the need for a lot of on-site intrusion of a target.

Interestingly, in addition to verifying the breadth and scope of the targeted city, I began to realize how many targets and their criticalities are reproduced literally in every city. Although I knew this before, I never fully realized how terrorists could hone their skills in one part of the world for a particular attack and a particular target, and then easily repeat that attack on a similar target in a city in a completely different area in the world by using remote surveillance collecting information online. Criminals do the same thing. We often read about legendary bank robbers that went across the country successfully robbing banks, yet we fail to realize that the criticalities, vulnerabilities, and avenues of approach are almost always the same in every bank, everywhere. The more citywide targets I looked at, the more similarities I discovered. This truly opened my eyes to how important it is to combine your online research with your on-site surveillance.

While my access and understanding was more advanced than the everyday civilian, I was profoundly awoken to what anyone with a computer and the ability to move around the outside of a targeted area can find. I took it upon myself to target a city where I lived, and then compare it to a city I would be traveling to in the near future, to see what kind of attacks could be repeated with minimal targeting of the second city, and just focusing on the standard sectors similarities. While I will not name the city, I think it is important to know that all cities (even the ones in other countries around the world) are basically cookie cutters of each other, just laid out in different arrangements. Every sector is represented in each city, and the criticalities of those sectors are basically the same. As the traffic road signs are primarily the same no matter where you go, so too are the sectors and their criticalities.

As I did this target package on these particular cities, I was able to see things so clearly via remote targeting that I was literally amazed at how much I knew when I showed up to do on-scene surveillance in my home city as well as the city I later visited. I specifically remember looking at the arenas where concerts and sports were played. When I was looking at the satellite images, you could see worn-down paths in the cement where everyone enters the building, and the same type of discoloration of where everyone exits at the same time at arenas in both cities.

In my home city, I went to a concert and watched all the people filter in on the paths I had noticed from a satellite image, and then watched everyone leave in the area I could clearly see online that was the main gate exit. Fascinating from a targeting perspective because I found the same thing happening at the stadium I visited in the second city. Based on that discovery, I was confident it would be the same in many stadiums around the country, and even around the world.

That discovery is what truly led me to write this book, because just as the targets and their criticalities are the same city to city, so too is the lack of awareness and empowerment of the people to defend themselves. While it may be true that we cannot change the cookie-cutter city structures around the world, we can change the people and give them more awareness as well as empowered tactics to make themselves as safe as possible. That empowerment starts with the research and discovery of general information.

History Is Really the Best Teacher

A Tactical Perspective

"History is the greatest teacher." While I'm not sure who exactly said it first, there have been many leaders and scholars that have uttered similar phrases when reflecting on issues past and present. Like many great sayings, this is mostly true, and there is plenty of evidence to support such a statement. So what does history teach us about facing and defeating past obstacles in today's modern world? And just as important, why do individuals, as well as local, state, and federal entities, all ignore history? The answers to those questions can be varied, yet they are mistakes that have been repeated over and over throughout history as one of the founding fathers of the United States pondered over 200 years ago.

George Washington once said, "The marvel of all history is the patience with which men and women submit to burdens unnecessarily laid upon them by their governments." While the game of politics has always been brutal, today we see increasingly extreme and sometimes barbaric ramifications of bad or incompetent policies and/or reactions (which is more often the only policy that exists).

While the United States still remains one of the greatest superpowers of all time, most U.S. National Security and Foreign Policies are based on reaction when dealing with groups that use the tactic of terrorism. A reoccurring thread in these reactions is to recruit a "coalition" of countries to help in the fight. However, most of the political decisions around the globe by world leaders are also largely reactionary and based on what is best for their political party, mixed with a sprinkle of what's good for their country or the coalition for that matter.

History tells us that actions always beat reactions. Law-enforcement, military and Special Forces communities live by this creed. Now, we see groups like ISIS and their goal of an Islamic Caliphate, abiding by this same creed of "action beats reaction." Yet this is nothing new as, throughout history, rising Islamic Caliphates have subscribed to this doctrine, and as was shown in the early 1900s with the systematic genocide of over 1.5 million Armenians, their action is, and always has been, domination by force.

What then does history teach us about dealing with the modern Islamic Caliphate?

1. Tactical decisions based on politics are not effective when fighting a driven enemy and can lead to unnecessary burdens on the U.S. citizenry.
2. Coalitions built by reactive politicians and not action-oriented tactical leaders will fail due to a lack of commitment by all parties.
3. Action beats reaction, no matter who is on offense and/or defense.

"That men do not learn very much from the lessons of history is the most important of all the lessons that History has to teach" (Aldous Leonard Huxley). This is absolutely true, and you should take this warning from Mr. Huxley to heart as we are currently seeing the rise of not only Fundamental Islam, but a resurgence of communism as well with groups like ANTIFA (Anti-Fascist), who are supported by many people in politics and media.

None of this is new, and in fact, history has shown repeated examples of the steps groups that want to subvert free nations have repeated all over the world. My good friend and fellow Navy SEAL "Drago" grew up in Poland and saw many identical tactics used by the communist leadership there in the 1980s as he is now seeing employed in the United States and other countries around the world. One of his biggest questions he asks is,

"Why don't people take history seriously and use it to protect their freedoms?"

Take these warnings to heart as you continue to put your individual target package together, and remember that if a government should start taking history into account for better defenses, you should probably do the same.

History is also a great teacher when learning about the tactics of a specific group of attackers. It is also a great predictor of how and why you could be specified as a target and who might target you. History is the primary section you will need to update periodically as the tactics of attackers change as they discover new and innovative ways to carry out their mission. After you complete a target package, it is helpful to try to identify which groups would typically attack the areas you have focused on. When doing this, break the groups down into categories such as terrorists (international and domestic), criminals, deranged attackers, and even subcategories such as criminal sex offenders, burglars, and pickpockets.

Once you have simplified the list of who traditionally attacks what, you can further research the historical tactics and techniques specific attackers use. Then, go back to your list of criticalities you put together and formulate the most likely attacks associated with specific critical assets, critical areas, and critical times. Also, you can get a very good idea as to what vulnerabilities these attackers could exploit and the avenues of approach they would take.

Let's take a look at specific areas of history you should cover.

Target History

New York City provides another good example of attack probability versus attack possibility. New York itself has a huge attack probability, as it is known to be one of the biggest terrorist targets in the world. Since New York has been attacked multiple times and carries a constant threat of future terrorist attacks, the attack probability and attack possibility are both 100-percent. However, specific businesses and locations within the city have varied probability and possibility of actually being the target, and these measurements will vary from time to time depending on evolving tactics and motivations.

For instance, when I initially set out to write this book, a fancy French restaurant on Manhattan's Upper East Side had a low probability on the targeting menu for a terrorist, and to my knowledge no French restaurant in Manhattan has ever been attacked by a terrorist, nor have terrorists typically planned attacks on obscure restaurants in most places around the world. Taking all this into account, the possibility of a terrorist attack on a French restaurant in Manhattan should have been low. However, as we saw throughout 2015 and 2016, obscure French targets had increasingly become a focus for Islamic jihadists around the world, and so the possibility of an attack on a French restaurant in New York City also increased even though there have been "no known credible threats" to specific restaurants in New York.

If you're still not clear, just remember this: Is an attack possible anywhere? *Yes*, it's possible. Do the statistics that show high or low probability of an attack always predict where and when an attack may happen? *No*, statistical numbers show likelihood but never give absolute predictive warning.

With this understanding of changing attack tactics and motivation, you can start to expand your knowledge of who and why specific aspects of your life could be targeted while pinpointing the types of attacks that could happen at specific locations. By simply taking into account the changing trends of attack history, you can in fact discover a tremendous amount about who and why someone or some group may attack a sector of your life. You can also determine changing trends of how attacks are carried out and what types of targets are trending. Now, if you make these discoveries, you can literally take this information, sit down at your computer, and gather as much information concerning all these angles of discovery. At the same time, if you are looking at this information from the attacker's mindset, you will start to see patterns of critical areas, critical times, vulnerabilities, and attackers' avenues of approach.

Historical Tactics

As technology and information evolves, tactical evolutions in areas such as types of weapons utilized, training and expertise of the attackers, and targets vary through history with all groups.

A good example of evolving tactics is the comparison of pre- and post-September 11, 2001 (9/11) hijackings of commercial airliners by Islamic fundamentalists. Prior to 9/11, the typical tactic consisted of taking over the plane and forcing it to land, followed by negotiations for a specific outcome. Most pre-9/11 hijackings ended in minimal casualties. However, the hijackers on 9/11 displayed an evolution in tactics when they actually crashed the planes using suicide attackers. Since that date, numerous individuals have attempted to blow up passenger airliners using techniques such as an underwear bomb and a shoe bomb. Regardless of whether the attacks were effective, this evolution in tactics showed the world that the era of hijacking and negotiating was over, and the era of making brutal statements by crashing or blowing up planes had begun.

With each different type of attacker, not only will the target be different; the tactics and techniques will also change or in some cases be completely different. Remember, identifying your critical areas, critical times, vulnerabilities, and avenues of approach for an attacker will allow you to set up proper defenses no matter what type of attack you are guarding against or if the attacker is using old or new tactics.

Historical Target Selection

Criminals usually target very specific people and places and seek to obtain very specific things. Sex crimes are usually targeted toward assaulting humans of specific gender or age, while bank robbers target particular buildings that hold and manage large amounts of cash. Terrorists can be motivated by religious or "moral" beliefs and have a much broader spectrum of targets to choose from. What is important for you to remember here is that bad guys have to protect their techniques before they are able to exploit others.

Petty criminals hone their skills as they grow up, committing increasingly bold crimes as they learn behaviors of the people they are targeting. On the other side of the bad-guy spectrum, Islamic jihadists will often project their changing tactics to the world by practicing them in the Middle East and North Africa before attempting to teach attackers and plan operations in European and westernized countries. Overlooking these projected tactics is one of the most perplexing failures of security experts, law enforcement, and the general public when it comes to building defenses. Every single attack in Europe and the

U.S. homeland has been carried out multiple times by Islamic attackers in their native regions as they honed their skills, yet the federal government, state and local authorities, and the press are always surprised by new types of attack techniques when they arrive at our doorstep.

Historical Anniversaries

History can also help us understand when an attack could occur by studying anniversary dates that may be significant to specific groups. For instance, September 11 is a tense date every year because it is the anniversary of the attacks on New York City and the Pentagon and has become a significant date for terror groups to announce threats or carry out attacks. It was September 11, 2012, for example, when the attacks took place at the U.S. compound in Benghazi, Libya.

Similarly, on April 19, 1993, the Bureau of Alcohol, Tobacco, and Firearms (ATF) and FBI were involved in a standoff with David Koresh, the leader of the Branch Davidians, in Waco, Texas, ending with a horrific fire that killed 76 people inside the compound. Two years later, on April 19, 1995, the Oklahoma City bombing carried out by Timothy McVeigh detonated a 5,000-pound ammonium nitrate bomb outside a federal building in Oklahoma City, killing 168 people and injuring more than 680. McVeigh purposely picked that date to coincide with the Waco incident because he had developed a great hatred of the U.S. government.

History shows us that the probability of an attack happening every September 11 or April 19 forever is actually very low; however, history has proven that it is absolutely possible, and those two dates hold significance to certain groups. Make note of these and similar historically "loaded" dates and be particularly cautious of any critical areas you are visiting on those days. I personally do not travel on either of those dates if at all possible. Some may think that is extreme, but unless someone attacks me at home or at the grocery store, I will remain safe if a repeat attack is carried out on September 11 or April 19.

Remember, history is the best way to determine the possibility of an attack on you and the different critical areas in your life. Evolving tactics, changing focus of attackers, advancements in technology, and important anniversaries are all important when finalizing the who, why, when, where, and how an attacker could strike.

Now let's move to another part of the information collection and look more closely at information verification, also called on-site surveillance. You will quickly see how well you know your locations, and you will start to realize that you already have an idea for the reality of everything in the attack package equation that you have gained through memory and remote surveillance.

What you will be attempting to do with on-site surveillance is verification of the planned attacks above in Step Five and the details of the criticalities that can only be verified with eyes on target.

CHAPTER 5

On-Site Information Verification and Collection

NOW THAT WE HAVE dissected the sector titled HOME in order to chart the general target information as well as historical threat information, you have a better understanding of where to begin with on-site information verification and collection. Even though it is your home and you are there every day, try taking the list in STEP FIVE of the target equation and walk around your home as if you were doing surveillance on it.

If your home is the one described in this exercise, you could get in your car and approach from the freeway to see how you might do surveillance in your neighborhood. When it is dark one night, go for a walk through the dry creek bed in the back yard and see what an attacker would see. Peer into your children's windows and see what an attacker would see. On a random night ask your family to sit inside and listen to see if they can hear or spot you sneaking around and looking in through a window. Are there creaks on the porch? Will the dog bark? Make it a game with the children and let the teenager know how serious of an exercise it actually is. When the kids are asleep, see how much noise outside it takes to wake them up. All of this, performed with the attacker's mindset, not the defender's, will help you verify what you have discovered about your home.

The same can be applied to other sectors of your life (although sneaking in places and peering in through windows is not suggested). This chapter speaks to exactly how you can build upon the information you've collected and charted, and, in many instances, it will help you see attack possibilities you may have overlooked.

Up Close and Personal

Even with the danger of getting caught, most attacks will at some point be preceded by target surveillance. Even with today's technology and computer mapping programs, ground surveillance is still a necessary step in building an accurate target package. As has been reported in the attacks on the Benghazi, Libya, diplomatic compound that killed U.S. Ambassador to Lybia, J. Christopher Stevens, information analyst Sean Smith, senior security operative Tyrone S. Woods, and security operative Glen Doherty, the attackers had apparently done extensive ground surveillance before the attack, including pacing off the distance from the targets to accurately fire mortars. The subsequent attacks displayed pinpoint accuracy in movement of attackers and mortar fire launched onto the two compounds.

Specific information is more difficult to obtain than the general information we discussed in Chapter 4. Information such as building layouts, accessibility, possible foot-surveillance locations, and best avenues of approach will be more difficult to obtain online and will require you to visit the target area in order to get a clear picture of these specifics. Initially collecting good general information will set you up for a better understanding of what you have to verify when on the ground.

In many cases, the specific information you can find online will surprise you, when you consider it from an attacker's point of view. For instance, many popular locations in cities around the world have webcams that show potential tourists exactly what it's like on a typical night at that location. Unfortunately, this is an excellent tool for attackers when they are developing a target package, as the critical times and critical areas are readily displayed for the entire world to see and take note of. Remember, as you work your way through this book, consider it also as an instruction manual for gaining awareness in order to build better defenses. The more you apply the techniques and thought processes to make your life safer, the less likely you are to find yourself in the middle of an attack.

Actually, being in and around the target area of interest is in fact the most dangerous area for the attacker prior to carrying out an attack. If they are spotted, or think that the awareness level is too high, there is a good chance they will find an alternative target. Surveillance will typically be done by attackers with advanced training, or by individuals with an agenda or specific location in mind. Generally, surveillance will be done multiple times. It can include dry runs where the attacker(s) run through their plan in real time at the location, or they might cause a disturbance to see how security/police respond. Nevertheless, anytime an attacker or a person collecting information moves in proximity to or actually on the location of a target, their own vulnerability grows. Make note of this when you see something suspicious or just when you have thought one of these scenarios through. Remember, just letting a potential attacker know they are being looked at or searched for could make all the difference in the world when securing a facility or yourself.

Ground surveillance is broken down into two categories: vehicle surveillance and foot surveillance. Please note that since we began discussing building a target package, we went from an outer circle of information collection and slowly moved inward, defining the target(s) and specific information needed to understand the critical areas, critical times, vulnerabilities, and avenues of approach.

Remember, *Sheep No More* is not written with the security professional in mind. It is written for an average person who wants to increase their awareness of who, why, where, when, and how an attack could happen. As such, the actual breakdown of the target-planning cycle is condensed from what someone like a Navy SEAL or law-enforcement officer might use.

Vehicle Surveillance (Close)

Vehicle surveillance can be conducted with minimal footprint on the target area and still give an attacker relevant knowledge. An attacker can gain knowledge of the police and security presence, the demographics of the population, escape routes, stand-off distances, and even the best avenues of approach for foot surveillance and the actual attack. Also, target proximity to roads, alternative targets, and the actual first-responder locations can be determined/affirmed by an attacker, giving them

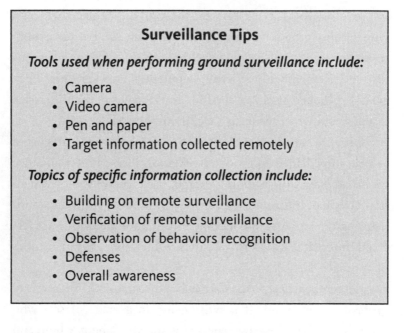

Surveillance Tips

Tools used when performing ground surveillance include:

- Camera
- Video camera
- Pen and paper
- Target information collected remotely

Topics of specific information collection include:

- Building on remote surveillance
- Verification of remote surveillance
- Observation of behaviors recognition
- Defenses
- Overall awareness

an adequate, almost complete understanding of their area of operations.

However, make no mistake about it: attackers can become so focused on obtaining information at this distance that they can give away their presence if a defender knows what to look for. I point this out because, as in the case of many VBIEDs against fixed targets, if the security force had been focused more on the activities around their facility, they may have been able to foil surveillance when it was at the vehicle stage. Most attackers that see this heightened awareness will pick another target.

If an attacker is not discovered after vehicle surveillance is conducted, the targeting planning will move even closer into the target area, leaving the comfort and security of the vehicle and putting people on the actual target when possible. From the defender's point of view, having a keen eye and a well-trained security/police force, along with an aware public, can be the greatest determining factor in whether an attack goes forward.

Foot Surveillance (Danger Close)

Foot surveillance brings the attacker into the personal space of the target and can verify a lot of the specific information an attacker is looking to gain on a target. Foot surveillance can determine the angle and focus of external and internal cameras. Building layouts that could not be gained online can also be studied, as can building structure. Depending on the type of attacker, surveillance performed on target can verify or determine the most critical areas and the most critical times for an attack. Criminal attackers, for instance, may not want large crowds present. For terror attacks, the opposite may be true. Critical assets can also be located and the vulnerabilities verified.

Taking notes on a target is not the only thing foot surveillance is about. An attacker can also perform mock attacks to determine pace and time on target, or they can cause incidents that will test the speed of the security/police reaction, identify where they stage, and reveal other crucial information.

At its essence, foot surveillance allows an attacker pinpoint information collection, but it comes at a cost. This same surveillance also allows the defender an opportunity to foil an attack and, if lucky, capture an attacker before the final stage of mission planning. Again, you can see the parallels between the attacker's and defender's perspectives and how learning about an attacker's mindset and focus will ultimately help set up the greatest potential defenses possible.

As I mentioned earlier in this chapter, behaviors, social dynamics, and routines in and around a target not only tell an attacker what they will need to wear, but they also tell an attacker and a defender what the racial breakdown of the population around the target represents, behaviors they should be aware of, and what is not normal in and around a certain area. It is then possible for attackers to mimic these specifics, while it makes it easier for defenders to use their specific identifiers to spot bad guys, as people foreign to a community will never fully be able to just fit in unless they live there for a time. Remember, considering race, fashion, behaviors, etc. does not make you a racist, bigot, or anything else. Realistically learning about a community in which you live, work, worship and play is normal and just, and it is analysis you will need to do in order to understand who is a threat and who is not in a particular sector of your life.

Behavior Recognition

Your Daily Routine

Places of work, educational venues, malls, and religious institutions are all examples of sectors that have been attacked in various ways throughout the United States. Understanding this statistic, you should be able to take the target-surveillance mindset and apply it anywhere in most daily routines, daytime or nighttime.

Your Family Routine

Adults, teens, and younger children all have different routines that can vary depending on where everyone is and what time they are there. The threats can be specifically broken down and targeted by individuals and/or groups that want to do harm. The critical areas and critical times will be very different for a child than for an adult, and even a teenager.

Once you identify these critical areas and critical times, as well as the vulnerabilities and avenues of approach that target surveillance might uncover, you can go through these different sectors of life and look at them from an attacker's point of view.

Workplaces, for instance, have high amount of foot traffic from 7:00 to 9:00 a.m. while people arrive. Another critical time could be 11:00 a.m. to 1:00 p.m., which is the typical lunch time when people congregate in the main areas of a building. The end of a work day, typically between 5:00 and 6:00 p.m., is when the majority of people will be grouped in one area as they leave work around the same time.

Many of these areas and times can overlap between family members in places such as malls, schools, and entertainment venues. Remember, when I point out the specific areas, times, and vulnerabilities, I am pointing out where the threat lies or the avenue of approach exists. As I have said several times so far the attacker and defender mindsets see things in a very similar way. Understanding this makes it much easier to flip back and forth between an attacker and defender perspective once you get comfortable with seeing things from an offensive and defensive stance. Likewise, your understanding of behavior recognition will improve, as long as you understand what is normal in and around every area of your life.

Specific Behavior Recognition

Let's take a look at a case study that stood out to me when I was a guest on Geraldo Rivera's show on Fox News shortly after I left the FBI in 2013. As you read this case study, think about how the family could have benefited by considering the information you have learned so far. If the Anderson family had done a target package on themselves, they could have considered the kids as critical assets and what type of attacker might have been drawn to those assets. Consider this, Hannah Anderson's abductor did his homework on his target before he slowly moved close to her, killed her family and kidnapped her.

Behavior Analysis: The Kidnapping of Hannah Anderson

On August 3, 2013, sixteen-year-old Hannah Anderson was abducted by forty-year-old James Everet Lee DiMaggio Jr., a close friend to the Anderson family, shortly after he murdered Hannah's mother and brother, Christina and Ethan Anderson, and the family's dog, Cali. The family members were discovered in the rubble of DiMaggio's home, which he burned before fleeing with Hannah. For a week, authorities searched for Hannah, until she was discovered on August 7 by some very aware individuals on horseback in Cascade, Idaho. Three days later, on August 10, FBI agents assigned to the Hostage Rescue Team (HRT) killed DiMaggio in a shootout near their campsite and rescued Hannah.

While this story is compelling in many aspects, it is important to understand that according to reports, DiMaggio had displayed some typical behaviors of a child predator. Unfortunately for the Andersons (as is the case with most people) the true nature of child predators and their cunning and patient tactics are largely unknown because people fail to recognize the prevalence of these manipulative attackers.

In comparison to the majority of attack case studies covered in this book, child predators typically do not rush in and kidnap a child or kill in a violent rage. Although this is sometimes the outcome of abduction, child predators will often engage a family through social means such as religious institutions or hobbies. Once the predator is introduced to the family, they will slowly work their techniques to gain trust and individual time alone with the child they have become fixated on. A good way to understand this process of gaining trust and proximity to an intended target, consider the tactics of a government intelligence operative that recruits spies from other countries versus a military special-forces operator that carries out direct action missions. Both can be considered attackers in their own unique way and in some cases (i.e., building and maintaining target packages on potential targets), their missions may overlap at times. However, the end game of a direct-action commando is to get in, attack, and get out, whereas the intelligence operative might utilize a source to carry out long term manipulative operations with a goal of not being discovered.

Similarly, in order to discover who, why, where, when, and how a child predator may slither into your surroundings in an attempt to slowly attack your child, you must understand their mindset and typical tactics and techniques. Even a brief search of typical child predator tactics on the internet can dramatically increase your ability, and the ability of your children to spot suspicious behavior. How do the FBI and CIA catch intelligence agents working against the United States? They study known tactics in spy craft that are commonly used in the intelligence world, and apply that knowledge by considering themselves as the target. Using this angle, they identify where their vulnerabilities are located and how they could be exploited, which allows the development of defensive tactics to counter any covert operations. This is exactly how you prepare your family for possible intrusion by a child predator or any other manipulative, slow-moving attacker.

Another interesting fact that we should point out about the Hannah Anderson case is the date of the death of the suspect's father, James Everet DiMaggio Sr., who committed suicide exactly eighteen years earlier to the day, August 10, 1995, following accusations of attempting to kidnap the sixteen-year-old daughter of an ex-girlfriend in 1988.

No one will ever know if the actions of DiMaggio's father had anything specifically to do with the date Hannah Anderson was abducted. Yet it is chilling to realize that, similar to terrorists and other predators, deranged attackers can be affected or motivated by previous actions of those around them, and, in fact, repeat deadly actions on anniversaries of previous attacks.

As you can see through the case study of Hannah Anderson, behavior recognition is basically an exercise in understanding the history of what is normal in a specific area or what is typical behavior of a specific type of attacker.

Although behavior profiling is one of the best defenses against attack, it is often misconstrued as one of the most controversial tactics. Because behavior analysis is constantly politicized and renamed profiling, people and agencies are reluctant to utilize its usefulness. However, if everyone in a specific community looks and dresses similarly based on the racial breakdown of the population and the latest fashion, the criminals will do their best to mimic their surroundings, and recruit individuals that fit that location's specific profiles. If that is the case, defenders should be able to do the same without worry of being accused of prejudice. As terrorists have shown around the world in their pre-attack planning and successful missions, using political correctness as a shield to operate under, is something they will readily exploit as often as they can. This is how attackers think and it is how they use the system to fit in as much as possible when doing pre-attack surveillance.

Actual behavior analysis goes beyond race, gender, and clothes. Humans doing something wrong inherently give off signals of behavior that do not fit within normal activities. This is because it is nearly impossible to accurately obtain information about a person, place, or thing without stepping forward and overtly collecting that information. There are very few people trained to do nefarious things without sending guilty signals as well.

Breaking down behavior analysis does not take a psychology degree, nor do you need to be an experienced law-enforcement officer. Simply paying close attention to what is typical behavior in and around your everyday life will give you enough knowledge to understand abnormal behaviors. In order to become proficient in behavior analysis, try looking closely at these four categories:

- Normal identifiable patterns of behavior
- Normal location of behavior
- Normal prolonged behavior
- Normal intrusive behavior

Behavior analysis involves analyzing not only behavior but also how normal behavior changes from location to location. People act differently in a mall than they do in church. Adults act differently at a major-league sports game than they do in and around a school. Adults picking up children at those schools act differently than the teachers and staff of those schools. Each location paints its own picture of what's normal for that location.

Similarly, there are lots of public bus stops located in proximity to schools. Normal behavior would allow for a person to wait for up to thirty minutes for a bus. Seeing a person at this same bus stop for three to five hours, and spending a lot of time watching the playgrounds, is not normal. However, because it's a public bus stop and it's not considered odd behavior to sit and wait there, most people would not take notice of a person that is there for a prolonged period.

Intrusive behavior is probably the least common but the most telling behavior that screams trouble. 99-percent of the time, someone who is trying to access a location that is locked or clearly states "No Entry" or "Emergency Exit" is trying to get somewhere they are not supposed to be. Regardless of whether this high percentage applies to residences (we all lock ourselves out at least once in our lives), you should not assume it's the resident when you see someone trying to get in without using the key in the front door. Intrusive behavior is, as its own name says, intrusive, and therefore is a behavior that is not normal and should be noted.

Target Package Completion

That is basically all you need to know about building an attack package for the sake of targeting yourself and your surroundings. If you take each sector of your life and systematically walk through the criticalities and the attacker histories (considering all the attacks we mentioned in Chapter 2) you will be more aware, more likely to avoid attacks, and more likely to survive if you are ever confronted with the reality of an imminent violent attack.

But building the target package is only half the technique of Attack and Defend. Now you have to flip the switch to defender so you can consider the defender's position and understand that it is just as powerful as the attacker's position. Chances are you will never be an attacker, so all of your actions will be focused on building defenses and thinking of your action beforehand so when the time comes for defense to turn to offense, you will respond with violence of action!

NOTE: AT THE END OF THIS BOOK SEVERAL BLANK PAGES WILL BE PROVIDED FOR YOU TO TAKE NOTES, MAKE SKETCHES AND LOG NORMAL AND ABNORMAL BEHAVIORS IN AND AROUND YOUR SECTORS.

PART 3

THE DEFENDER

Now that we have completed a target package and you have learned exactly how attackers think and how they explore your life for answers to the attack equation, you can see that this accumulated information can be used by an attacker or defender.

Information collection can be general or specific and it can be collected remotely on a computer or on-scene using vehicle or foot surveillance. All of this information ultimately helps the attacker determine who, why, when, where, and how the best place for an attack will be, and that is the point at which you can flip the switch and start looking for ways to firm up and harden your own defenses.

Believe it or not, what you have seen compiled so far using this attacker's mindset is the exact same information security experts use to develop a proper defensive strategy. There is no need for you to log more information or create special charts. If you are a civilian, all you need to do is set standards in place to mitigate or eliminate your exposure to critical areas and times and establish standard operating procedures to act in areas that you can't avoid but may be critical. While I do suggest that you take the time to write down these SOPs for your family to ensure they maintain full awareness, I realize this may not be a realistic demand and that many people, young and old, simply will not take the time to develop SOPs for safety. Funny thing, many people that have seen a scary movie about old houses and/or scary clowns will actually, subconsciously, set up SOPs for avoiding both old houses and clowns. So, when presenting the results of your target package to family, friends, and coworkers, make sure you drive home the result of not being prepared. As you can see, I'm not above a little bit of scare tactics when needed. However, the most important part of this technique is visualizing the attack, which we have done. If you can instill in people enough detail about who, why, where, when, and how an attack can happen, they will visualize what you are telling them and you all will already be miles ahead of anyone who wants to attack.

Forging

Honing these defenses and going back and forth between the polar-opposite mindsets is similar to ancient sword making. For instance, ancient samurai swords were heated up and folded hundreds of times before they were honed into a razor-sharp weapon that could be used to cut a human being in half with one powerful and precise cut. Over and over the master swordsmith heats, folds, hammers, and then cools the steel, only to repeat the process. This is called forging, and the same principle applies to building your defenses: constantly working, evaluating, and perfecting your plans until you have a solid product. This forging of your defenses allows them to become stronger and stronger where needed, it helps define what works and what doesn't, and it identifies vulnerabilities that may be created by the implementation of new defenses. Yes, that's correct—new defenses often create new critical areas and critical times, vulnerabilities, and even new avenues of approach.

CHAPTER 6

Defender Mindset

As a SEAL, I was trained as an attacker using unconventional tactics and thinking. I knew that if I were surveilling a target and I was spotted, I would either walk away and come back another day to attack, or we would abandon the tactical mission altogether and look for an alternative technology or target to achieve the same outcome. We made these decisions based on years of testing and real-world missions that determined what our SOPs would be on target.

Likewise, SEALs and other special forces teams use the intelligence collected on the enemy's SOPs to target gaps in their awareness and security. As an FBI Special Agent in charge of developing threat assessments on potential targets, I used this attacker (offensive) mindset to help pinpoint gaps in security that other law-enforcement representatives could not see because they did not have the training or experience in unconventional thinking.

As I am bound by my oath to protect the classified information I was tasked with while serving in these various agencies and programs, I can only cover certain parts of what I did in the FBI. However, without giving any specifics about how I used my technique of Attack and Defend, I can tell you that it provided me great insight on numerous occasions, including my prediction that an Islamic attacker would place a car bomb in Times Square in the vicinity of the Marriott Hotel over a year before Faisal Shahzad did just that on May 1, 2010. That Saturday evening, Shahzad parked his recently purchased 1993 Nissan Pathfinder on a side street next to the Marriott and just above a packed theater of patrons watching a performance of *The Lion King*. I was the second FBI Special Agent on scene and I immediately started feeding information to the FBI's Joint Terrorism Task Force for investigators while I coordinated responding assets.

The entire time I was there that night and into the evening I wanted to shout, "I told you so!" There it was in plain sight, a VBIED placed exactly where I had said it would be, by the exact people I said would put it there. How did I reach this conclusion over a year before it happened? Like many other individuals that had performed threat assessments in and around New York City, I had looked at things from an attacker's point of view. However, what differentiated my threat assessments was that I had been paying close attention to the changing shift in tactics being used by Islamic attackers overseas and also specific fixations that kept popping up creating patterns that most people just discounted. There had started to be a shift from grand attacks like the 9/11 hijackings to more and more VBIEDs and gun attacks in the Middle East, most specialists recognized this shift. However, there was also a recurring fixation with the Marriott brand that kept popping up from time to time in various attacks overseas.

When I looked at the evolving tactics of killing less, publicizing more, I saw no better place for an attack than Times Square, and when I combined that with the fixation on Marriott, I started to see the attack picture unfold. I knew, based on my training and experience and my technique of Attack and Defend, that there was a high possibility (not probability, although that was high as well) that individuals overseas directing attacks against the United States could choose the busy intersection exactly where Faisal Shahzad parked his 250-pound bomb that fortunately failed to detonate.

Faisal Shahzad actually succeeded in many ways, although his attack fizzled because of errors in the steps he took to build the bomb. While he may have failed the explosives class given by attack planners, he did not fail at surveillance, target selection, and choosing a vehicle that wasn't flashy; had the bomb gone off, he actually might have been able to escape. Fortunately for us, his bomb didn't ignite, giving the incredible investigators on the Joint Terrorism Task Force the investigative keys they needed to quickly track the purchase of the Nissan Pathfinder to the person he bought it from, which led to his capture as he sat on a plane getting ready to depart the country.

Although we love to turn foiled attacks into victorious news in this country, the Faisal Shahzad incident should not be considered a complete victory. In fact, the victory lies with the FBI investigators and NYPD detectives who located him after the attack. Identifying him before the attack was a complete failure that is largely due to bad political policies and old Standard Operating Procedures (SOP).

If you are a mayor, you should be asking the chief of police, "What are our SOPs?" If you are a facility manager, you should be asking your director of security, "What are our SOPs?" If you are an individual, with or without a family, you should be asking yourself, "What are my SOPs?" Is it clear to you that I am trying to drive home the term "standard operating procedures"? In order to live a carefree life, you either have to walk around in a clueless stupor or you must develop SOPs so that structured awareness exists. Otherwise you are a sitting duck for bad guys with all kinds of motivations to attack.

By looking at yourself and your surroundings from an attacker's point of view, you will have 90-percent of the technique completed so you can defend against potential attacks and make educated reactions when you are at the wrong place at the wrong time. Next time you are at the grocery store and you see fresh fish for sale, remember this: 75-percent of the earth is covered by water. Those fish had literally millions of miles to swim and live, yet they ended up in the wrong place at the wrong time. *Don't be the fish!* Likewise, joggers that were injured at the Boston Marathon bombing in 2013 had run 26.2 miles just to end up exactly where a terrorist bomb was detonated. Always be aware, knowing your critical areas, critical times, vulnerabilities, and attackers' avenues of approach.

Whether you realize it or not, you have learned enough since you started reading this book to go back and forth between the attacker and defender mindsets. You also have an understanding of how well you can build a defense by knowing who, why, where, when, and how an attack could be carried out against you or your surroundings. Being unaware of your surroundings and not having a plan to respond are actually two different issues, but both are based on a lack of understanding of the target package an attacker will develop.

Remember, I don't just play the part of an expert who knows a lot about security, as is the case with so many people in the security field today. My years of experience have instilled in me a targeting mentality that allows me to look at situations not only as a defender, but also as a tactician of targeting. I pride myself on having climbed the ladder of success in the special operations arena, then climbing another ladder to the top law-enforcement agency in the world.

Why do I point out my resume and repeat the depth and focus of my experience again? Because I want you to realize that despite all my years of training and operating, if I wanted to effectively attack you, I'd have to learn what you already know about your surroundings. That's right: *you* hold the key to *your* own defenses. No matter how experienced, tough-looking, or credentialed a security expert or attacker may be, they must gain the knowledge you, the defender, have in order to attack or defend you. From a targeting perspective, it is much easier and cheaper for me to show you how to understand your knowledge than it is for you to pay an "expert" to wing it.

As we have discussed, knowing who, why, where, when, and how an attack may happen is the result of a well-rounded attack package, and it is the culmination of information collection that an attacker will need in order to plan an effective attack. In order to establish and test these defenses, you will need to master the technique of flipping the switch between the mindset of an attacker and a defender, going back and forth and evaluating the reality and effectiveness of your defensive ideas.

All of what we have done so far can be accomplished without spending a single dollar. Time and attention to detail are your biggest investments. Having this benefit of understanding and insight will allow you as an individual, company, or public entity (i.e., city, state, or federal agency) to not only control your security budget, but actually develop an understanding of your critical areas, critical times, vulnerabilities, and attackers' avenues of approach better than most so-called "security experts."

I know it is hard to believe, but most of the people in charge of setting up domestic defenses for the United States are not trained in unconventional thinking. In fact, I was once yelled at by a senior FBI Special Agent for thinking outside the box too much. His exact words were, "Do you know what your problem is? 90-percent of the ideas you come up with are outside of the box! This is the FBI—90-percent of what we do is inside the box." Unknowingly, that agent had just given me one of the biggest compliments of my career and validated exactly what being an effective attacker and defender is all about. (Thank you, Benny.)

With this new skill, you will be able to quickly identify all of your criticalities and develop actions for a quicker, more accurate, and potentially life-saving response for you and those you love if you end up in the arena of an attacker.

Simplicity is the key, and you must realize that there is no need for you to complicate this process by focusing on what others may say is or is not a target. You are not planning a specific mission to attack like a SEAL, so you do not have to go that far into the attack package in order to figure out the criticalities of each sector of your life. However, as you study the scenarios in the following chapters, you will start to sharpen the skills needed to see the world as a series of soft areas and criticalities. In essence, the better you understand these few short techniques, the faster you can flip the switch between attacker and defender.

The important thing to remember is that the more you play this game, the faster you will become at discovering the probability of an attack occurring where you will be, and you will be better prepared to act, not just react. But you must start with the attacker's mindset first.

A Defensive State of Mind

While consulting with one of my clients who owned several hotels, we were discussing the rise in crime in and around all their hotels, with one hotel reporting higher numbers of robberies and burglaries in and around the property. These hotels were in highly respected and well-regarded locations, and the owner was afraid that the increase in crime was already taking a toll on patrons. After we discussed the issues, I led the owner and a few of his managers through some awareness training. About a quarter of the way through the training, I asked the managers to pick one person from each area of the hotel staff to join in the discussion. As the discussion continued, I briefly covered the concepts of critical areas, critical times, vulnerabilities, and avenues of approach.

Once the group understood these simple concepts, we pulled up what information we could find on the internet and did a basic remote surveillance, allowing us to see what others could use to plan attacks of a criminal nature. After that, we all walked the perimeter of the hotel, taking turns talking about when, where, and how suspect criminals were able to get into the hotel and carry out the attacks. After the perimeter tour and a brief stroll through the interior of the hotel, we returned to the conference room and assumed the role of the bad guys, discussing where we would be able to effectively carry out surveillance, when this surveillance would get best results, and how the surveillance would help us predict vulnerable areas before we actually set foot on the property. Next, we discussed where the best place to attack would be for a robbery or room break-in.

Lastly, we took what we had discussed, charted it on a diagram of the compound layout, and reversed our roles to defenders. Using the ideas we had come up with as a group, we started to see the unique view each person brought to the table. The bellmen saw things differently than the maintenance staff. The managers saw things differently than the housekeepers, and the night auditor saw things differently than everyone! These unique views helped us discover and fully understand the hotel's different vulnerabilities.

After about an hour discussing the different ways to defend the property from criminals, we agreed on three main tactical defenses:

First, instead of pointing all the cameras at areas deemed important, such as the lobby, we turned the cameras toward the avenues of approach that an attacker might come from. These avenues were also the direction in which surveillance would most likely be carried out, giving us an initial and secondary chance to catch suspicious behavior.

Second, we realized that doors in and around this massive complex had card readers to allow patrons to enter after daylight hours at locations closer to their rooms. In response, the hotel turned off these card readers after dark and placed signs above the doors reading, "For your safety, all patrons must enter through the front entrance after dark. Thank you for your understanding." This eliminated any chance that criminals would be able to pose as another guest and piggyback through a remote door that a patron had scanned to get in. Criminal activity was low in these areas during the daytime because they were so busy with guests and staff coming and going, but the doors were deemed to be highly critical areas at night. And thus, that criticality was mitigated.

Third, a poll was taken among the employees and it was found that half of the staff smoked. When taking a smoke break, the employees would typically do so in the dock area located in the rear of the hotel compound. Often employees would take breaks together, whether they smoked or not. Because the budget did not allow hiring more security officers, a security booth was placed at the dock area, and employees were required to walk the perimeter of the building while they smoked or just took a break. These employees were told about the critical areas and most likely avenues of approach a criminal might take to get into the facility. Instead of just randomly walking, the employees were instructed to simply look in the direction of the avenues of approach as they walked. This allowed an almost continuous roving patrol with eyes on the avenues of approach for a criminal. And as we discussed, most people with nefarious intentions will pick another target if they believe the awareness around a place of interest is too high.

As a result of these three simple changes in all of the client's hotels, theft in and around the hotels virtually stopped. Because all the employees had been given a little bit of awareness training, they became more aware not only while walking the perimeter but also throughout the day in their regular routines. The management, which had trained alongside the staff, began to take issues that the staff brought up more seriously, which in turn empowered the staff because they felt trusted. It was an incredible circle of awareness and professionalism that allowed for a safer environment and a more hardened target for criminals to penetrate.

Just as impressive was the increase in return customers because of the safe and professional feeling they got when staying at the hotels. Not only had these three simple changes made real proactive differences in safety, it actually profited the company tremendously in the end.

In contrast to a large company's lack of awareness, the individual person must also realize they are the master of their own homeland and that it is the individual who holds the key to the safe that is full of the information about their critical areas, critical times, vulnerabilities, and attackers' avenues of approach.

On this individual and local level, most people make the same mistake in believing or pretending they are very aware and understanding of who, why, where, when, and how an attack may occur. As you will see in this short case study told to me by the victim's friend, a false sense of security is rooted in complacency. After you read this story, think about the systematic thinking that the attackers used to pick a target, a location for the attack, and their escape route. You will see that they basically created a target package. Although the victim may have been randomly chosen, the game is anything but random as those individuals or groups of individuals that consciously knockout unsuspecting people for a thrill will most likely have an agenda and a plan.

Also, as you read the story, remember that it is not made up. It really happened to a real person, and then imagine if that were you or one of your loved ones. How could it have been avoided? Could the type of attack, the location and time of the attack, the nationality or race of the potential attacker, their motivation for attacking, and their avenue of approach actually have been predicted? The answer is yes. Remember, this book is not a discriminatory or politically correct publication. It is reality, and when I ask the question, "could you predict the nationality or race of the attacker," it is a statement based on statistics and locations, not predetermined judgments.

As I have said before, when you are building a target package on yourself you should take all the information available into account and set aside political and social pressures to disregard the statistics of violent offenders that may mention race, locations as well as other collected facts. I am not concerned with offending the people that most likely will not be there to rescue you from an attackers web. I am giving you this insight to teach you how to save your own life regardless of skin color, gender, sexuality, or any other unique characteristic. As you go through the rest of this book, I will cover these targeting characteristics in greater detail. So always remember, this book was written to empower everyone, so they may increase their likelihood of avoiding death or serious bodily injury from and attacker.

The Knockout Game

It is not uncommon to hear about people falling victim to a violent fad called the "knockout game." As barbaric and vicious as an attack by wild dogs, groups of young adults will stalk an unaware victim and attempt to knock them out with one punch, then run away. Because most people consider the probability of being attacked as about the same odds as winning the lottery, their awareness against such an attack is predictively low. But, as I always tell the lottery naysayers, someone eventually wins, and your odds of winning are as good as anyone else's.

In one incident, a middle-aged male was waiting for a train in New York City at one of its many subway stations. Even though the victim rode this train every day from this same station, and usually stood in the same place at the end of the platform, he had inadvertently backed himself into a corner where he was subsequently knocked out and severely beaten before the gang of attackers fled. Unfortunately, we can positively say that a lack of awareness of his everyday surroundings and not knowing the possibility or types of attacks that could happen in a New York subway station were the biggest contributing factors of the victim unknowingly isolating himself in a vulnerable area where attacks had previously occurred.

This is representative of the second-biggest mistake in awareness among security officials, law enforcement, military, and even individual civilians. Simply believing that you are secure and resting on confidence instead of proof is a correctible vulnerability that bad guys always look for.

At this point in the book you should be starting to develop an understanding of how attackers pick targets and how their plans usually involve more than just finding someone to attack. You should also be developing an eye for the particular focus attackers have for critical areas, the critical times for those areas, the vulnerabilities of the targets, and the avenues the attackers could take. Take, for instance, the attackers in the knockout game case study. Those attackers understood that the end of the subway platform was the best place to knock someone out because the target couldn't run away, and the cameras would probably not identify their actions if they pushed the victim close enough to the end. The attackers chose a time when it was moderately busy so their actions could be hidden and they had most likely predetermined which way to run based on their familiarity with that area. Now imagine if the attackers are backed by a rogue nation or an ideological powerhouse that wished to attack your city and kill as many people as possible. Imagine how detailed their attack plan would be, and consider what vulnerabilities they would find useful.

Guarding Against False Experts and Defensive Failures

True defenses, as you should have discovered by this point, are not based on budget and opinions or subscribing to a mantra of "I don't want to live in fear." Living in a state of oblivion or ego is dangerous and foolish. Between 2002 and 2005, I worked as a security specialist for a company named AMTI that was run by former members of the U.S. Navy SEALs, Army Special Forces, Army Rangers, Marine Corps, Air Force Special Operations, and Coast Guard. While at AMTI, I was lucky enough to be a part of two very successful Department of Homeland Security programs.

The DHS Site Assist Visit (SAV) program, as it was known then, enlisted the ranks of these former operators to identify and visit different private sectors of our national infrastructure determined to be soft targets. Teams of operators (called assault forces) were assigned to tall buildings, special events, malls, religious facilities, stadiums and arenas, and other specifically chosen locations so they could literally target the facility or event from an attacker's point of view. Afterward, the team would offer briefings so the locations could utilize our after-action reports to upgrade their security or, as was often the case, actually create proper defenses against attack.

Time after time, security was the last subject considered by most of the sectors that we met with. Most sectors considered law enforcement as their primary security, and the thought of spending money on something they could not predict would happen with absolute certainty was ridiculous.

I began to realize that the most common reason for a lack of security was financial and the second most common reason was ego. I understood the financial barriers, as most places we worked with had a finite budget based on their business projections. The same issues of money and funding were present in all of the religious facilities, whose budgets were based on collections and donations that limited spending across the board. But I was astonished time and time again with the breakdown of security across this nation due to the ego of managers, police chiefs, mayors, governors, members of the House of Representatives and the Senate, and even the Office of the President of the United States. My astonishment was further enhanced by what I had seen in the Federal Air Marshal Service and later as an FBI Special Agent in the New York office.

There were individual groups in the areas where we worked who were not ego-driven and legitimately asked how they could possibly afford the corrections in security needed to fill the gaps they now understood existed. The first thing we would recommend was teaching awareness to all the employees by sharing the information we had pointed out about critical areas, critical times, vulnerabilities, and attackers' avenues of approach. We suggested training employees to pay close attention to behaviors, identifying what was normal and what was not, and if they did have technologies such as cameras, we discussed their most effective use by targeting critical areas to identify anyone displaying odd behavior in those areas so the company could be alerted in the case of pre-attack surveillance.

What we emphasized the most at each location we visited was that an attacker *will* be looking to gain the basic knowledge of the facilities that they themselves already have—current security measures, shift changes, area access, and so on—and how we hoped they would guard against outside sources discovering their unique issues. Unfortunately, as far as I could tell, few suggestions were ever taken to fruition and awareness was never increased.

The second project I worked on while at AMTI was the Soft Target Awareness Training (STAT) program. When I was given this program to run, it was, by and large, a critical response program to connect the private and public sectors in the United States with first responders so they could prepare for the aftermath of an attack. Basically, the course had been designed by firefighters and first responders that did not have an understanding of the true potential of the course. They were reaching many people, but without instructing them on the most important part of securing our nation: identifying who the attackers are, why they would be a target, and where, when, and how they might be attacked.

Immediately I saw the need for an adjustment to this course so I began to make changes in order to bring what we had developed in the SAV program to the next level. You've heard of the phrase, "It's better to beg for forgiveness than to ask for permission." Well, that's exactly what I did. I pushed the envelope of what we call "political correctness."

Both the SAV program and the STAT course were part of a presidential review that kept close watch over the number of attendees and sectors we taught. At one point, an undersecretary of education (I forget her name) attended the course when I was teaching it in Fairfax, Virginia. I was excited that someone with clout was attending; however, this excitement was quickly extinguished because, as she put it in her letter complaining to DHS, the course was teaching individuals to become attackers and was designed more for military soldiers and was unfit for the civilian population.

Now, I cannot remember the exact words of that letter, but what I do remember is that there were several grammatical errors, including some misspelled words. I realized then, in my first experience with a political appointee, that many people in positions of authority know nothing about the things they criticize and just a bit more than nothing about the specialty in which they claim to be an expert. Because I had only been out of the SEAL Teams for a few years, my only other experience with this type of bureaucratic incompetence was in the leadership of the Federal Air Marshal Service, where egos ruled and common sense and reasoning were in short supply.

I later saw even more incompetence in the FBI leadership and, most of all, in our mainstream media, where political wonks and "experts" with little to no experience, understanding, or knowledge exist unchallenged. Concerning the media, it is not uncommon for the public to tune into a breaking-news event of terrorism and see a journalist, political appointee, or former high-ranking official pontificating on the situation, all of whom have zero experience in military or law-enforcement operations, analyzing terror attacks, or national security issues.

Even the former high-ranking officials you see on television are usually not from an operational background, and, coincidently, they are the same non-operators that have been leading our broken government agencies. They are often administrative functionaries who got their rank through some type of successful special project or political connection. Next time you see an important breaking-news event, write down the names of the panel members and see if any of them have experience in the subject they are analyzing. Don't just take a title of "former Assistant Secretary of Homeland Security" or "General" as all the evidence you need. See what they actually did to get that title and what they did when in that job. More often than not, you will see zero experience in unconventional warfare or targeting, and, therefore, zero knowledge or understanding that would make them capable of making suggestions on how to handle or respond to specific situations.

It is important to note that this book is not intended to be a series of complaints, but I do feel it is important for you to realize that no one will ever protect you better than you. Just like any profession, first responders, national security protectors, and governmental authorities, will often fall short of their intended objectives and, as far as security is concerned, they will never fully be able to protect you. These authorities can't tell you what is best for you on a daily basis so that you can live the life you choose. Most will not be there when any particular sector of your life is attacked or suffers chaos, and they won't solve most major issues in the world before they become big problems, especially in your immediate life. What they can do is tell you statistics, make suggestions about what to do after something happens, and respond after the crisis has already begun.

With this understanding of how authorities most often wait until post attack times to evaluate security for effective defenses, try to envision yourself as the attacker and defender as you read these next two case studies. Flip the switch back and forth in order to identify vulnerabilities the attackers focus on to plan an attack and how the defenders could focus on the same things to build better defenses. In doing this, remember that both incidents involve real life attackers that meticulously planned their attacks by formulating attack packages and using them to identify multiple mistakes that they could exploit in order to carry out effective attacks. You will see that those mistakes made by authorities and unsuspecting citizens were very common and are unfortunately still shared by individuals and agencies alike. The attackers knew that then, and modern-day attackers know it now as well. Also, ask yourself how you would log this information in an attack package from the attacker's point of view in order to keep track of all the criticalities that could be exploited and how you could use it to set up better defenses.

1999 Columbine School Attack and 2016 Pulse Nightclub Attack

Prior to 1999, the attack probability on a school in Columbine, Colorado, was virtually nonexistent. In fact, the probability for attack on *any* public school was considered so low that authorities around the country gave very little thought toward defenses at schools based on who might actually attack, how authorities could identify them, and where, when, and how someone might carry out such an attack. Regardless of the low probability, the 100-percent possibility was recognized when two deranged attackers planned and carried out an elaborate attack on Columbine High School on April 20, 1999.

Two senior students at the school, Eric Harris and Dylan Klebold, murdered twelve students and one teacher, while injuring twenty-one additional people, before taking their own lives in a suicide pact. For over a year, Harris, the psychopathic leader, and Klebold, the depressive follower, worked to acquire firearms, build bombs, and develop an elaborate attack mission plan that included an attack package on the high school and specific understandings of critical areas, critical times for those areas, and the vulnerabilities they could exploit to hit the soft areas. They paid particular attention to the avenues of entry/ exit for students inside the cafeteria and the avenues of approach that would be used by first responders. Homemade bombs were placed in all those locations. (Most failed to detonate.) Overall, Harris and Klebold possessed ninety-nine bombs of various sizes, four different guns, and four knives—they were prepared. There is evidence from the journals left behind by both boys that great consideration was placed on the lack of awareness and lack of understanding of possible attacks on the school by faculty, staff, and local authorities.

Because of the very low probability of an attack, the school was not prepared and law enforcement was caught off guard, causing a 100-percent reactive response. Because of this incident and the reaction to it, law-enforcement officials around the country became more proactive in their understanding that responding officers must address active shooters immediately. This led to the development of the basic active shooter training that most law-enforcement officers obtain, which, even though it is proactive in its vision, is still a completely reactive tactic. Regardless, it represented a shift in the understanding of probability numbers versus the possibility of an attack in the education sector.

Now that numerous attacks have happened all over the country at schools and universities, law enforcement should have shifted to an even more proactive stance in order to prevent attacks before they happen and develop a deeper understanding for their officers and the community's citizenry so they are more aware and ready to act in the case of an attack actually happening. Columbine set the shift in motion from training that focused on what the probability of an attack could be to an overall mindset that attacks are possible anywhere at any time. As the average number of injuries for school shootings grows, it should be apparent that a further, more proactive shift in law-enforcement tactics should start to take place. As of the publication of this book, this shift has not happened.

Fast-forward seventeen years and you see similar mistakes made by the Orlando Police Department when an Islamic attacker entered the Pulse nightclub in Orlando, Florida, and began shooting on June 12, 2016, at approximately 2:00 a.m. Although it was not a school, police were faced with a similar type of active-shooter attack but failed to neutralize the shooter quickly using direct-action tactics that had been developed as an outcome of the Columbine attack. Although the six responding officers initially followed active-shooter policies, the officers were told to hold their positions as the shooter barricaded himself in a bathroom with hostages. Shortly after being told to hold their position, the six officers inside the club were pulled out as

SWAT arrived and took over the scene. When asked why the officers inside the club were pulled out, Orlando police chief John Mina stated the scene had gone from an active-shooter to a barricaded-gunman scenario and that the shooter had hostages. Regardless of statistics that show mass shooters do not negotiate in this day and age, especially ones that call local television stations pledging allegiance to ISIS, the decision was made to have police negotiators speak with the shooter in an attempt to end the standoff.

As most military special forces operators will tell you, a firefight must be resolved before you begin rescuing people. As you can see, the aggressive mindset of special forces is one of the reasons they are so successful at rescuing hostages and killing bad guys in fluid situations. This understanding of triaging a fluid situation has not been fully comprehended by most police departments around the world, and both the Columbine and Orlando shootings show the breakdown of competent leadership as well as how police departments refuse to incorporate new, battle-tested tactics.

Most active-shooter attacks in the United States last around three minutes before police arrive on scene and the shooter is either killed by police or commits suicide, yet Orlando police pulled the officers out of the nightclub even though they were actively engaging the shooter and started using SWAT operators to clear the dead and wounded from inside the building, neglecting the proven tactic of aggressively pursuing the shooter until he is eliminated. Instead of three minutes, the Pulse nightclub shooting went on for three *hours* and ended with forty-nine victims slaughtered by the shooter before police killed him. At least five of the victims were killed inside the bathroom where the shooter had taken up a barricaded position.

The Orlando attack was terrorism, as the gunman used mass shooting to intimidate the citizenry and espouse a fundamental Islamic ideology of global domination. However, even though the motivation was different from Harris and Klebold during the Columbine attack, in both case studies forward thinking by the authorities was inadequate because they relied on outdated policies that encompassed ineffectual smoke-and-mirrors tactics aimed at negotiating an outcome with the shooters.

The days of negotiations during an active-shooter scenario are over—plain and simple. Any police department that fails to realize this is guilty of inadequate forward thinking about attacks and is gambling with the safety of their communities.

Offensive attackers seek out knowledge of the true abilities of the first responders in order to create a better, more realistic target package, and, likewise, you should take into account how an attacker could use these self-inflicted vulnerabilities of law enforcement, city officials, and private businesses to develop a more specific plan. The more weaknesses you are able to discover, the more you can target specific critical areas and critical times, which will lead you to an understanding of obvious types of attacks and their outcomes.

Stop and Frisk

Politicians and government officials routinely make these types of mistakes as we saw in Columbine and Orlando. For instance, consider the controversial "stop and frisk" technique also known as a "Terry Stop" utilized by the New York City Police Department (NYPD). "Stop and frisk" was based on the 1968 United

States Supreme Court Case of *Terry v. Ohio, 392 U.S.* that allows police officers to perform a limited detention and search of a suspect's outer garments based on articulable and reasonable suspicion that an individual may be armed and dangerous. As such, the NYPD had allowed officers to briefly detain a person on reasonable suspicion of involvement in criminal activity but short of probable cause to arrest.

Although many activists and politicians railed against this technique, they failed to take into account the proven results of active displays of awareness and forward thinking, and as a result, put their officers deeper in harm's way while putting the public at a greater risk of attack by creating an even greater vulnerability to the city of New York. By simply having the threat of officers searching at any time, bad guys' concerns of getting caught with a weapon increased. In theory, you would assume that many bad guys decided to no longer carry concealed weapons when they were in public, at mass transit sites, or at special events, all of which have a heightened police presence.

What the city of New York could have done was simply draw back on the number of permissible Terry stops without informing the public and leaving the sense of heightened aware-ness in place. Yes, this is smoke and mirrors, but it is based on real actions by law enforcement. Of course, from time to time the city would have had to press forward and increase the number of Terry stops for a period of time, displaying the continued tactic for continued effectiveness. But instead, politicians and NYPD officials caved to pressure and eliminated the tactic in a very public fashion, sending an open invitation to potential attackers that they could carry a concealed weapon without fear of search while in and around New York City.

Flipping the switch back to an attacker's mindset, you can now see how easy it is for bad people to identify vulnerabilities (weaknesses) they can exploit. The city of New York has literally made it easier for an attacker to carry out a mass shooting in a populated area by publicly eliminating the stop and frisk tactic.

All of the case studies covered in this chapter so far should give you a good idea of what indicators are and how attackers monitor politics, current events, and the awareness of citizens and authorities. All of these indicators are what you will start to notice as your thinking shifts to the attacker mindset, then flips back to a defensive posture. This will strengthen the foundation of your target package as well as reinforce your actual defensive SOP's, eliminating useless traditional defensive theatrics.

Defensive Theatrics

I recently watched a video on YouTube of former Delta Force operator Pat McNamara talking about shooting-range theatrics. If you haven't seen Pat's videos, you should watch some even if you are not a shooter, because he's a good example of an expert who knows how to communicate with individuals who think they know a lot but don't, as well as individuals who just haven't learned yet.

Pat's video made me pause because I have seen the same issues in the field of security, with defensive theatrics performed every day by people who should actually know better and many people in positions of authority that they aren't quite qualified to be in. Sadly, as Pat put it, "institutional inbreeding" is one of the biggest enablers of security theatrics. These dog and pony shows are actually rehearsed in many cases, with law-enforcement and security managers participating in mock attacks and drills. I cringe when I see police officers that haven't been trained properly clearing a facility in active-shooter scenarios. Then when SWAT arrives, I see the same outdated and useless tactics being performed, with the only difference being they are wearing much more gear.

Individuals often make the same mistakes and default to defensive theatrics. If you are a female, alone and walking into your apartment late at night, and you see a shady individual approaching you, and you say in a stutter, "You better leave me alone because I have pepper spray," they are probably going to see straight through this attempt to counter their attack. They know that someone with a defensive plan would have either scanned the area before they got out of their car, or they would have already had the pepper spray out, ready to use it. The attacker sees through these theatrics because effective attackers understand the history, normal behaviors, critical areas, critical times, typical vulnerabilities, and best avenues of approach, all of which have usually been tested in similar circumstances with other targets.

Some security theatrics can actually work if they are specifically chosen and actually used for a tactical advantage. At a shopping mall I visited when I was working as a security specialist, I saw a good example of defensive theatrics purposely used while full well knowing it was an illusion. They had a problem in their mall where drug dealers had set up shop and were easily selling to people because of the expansion of the facility and the number of patrons that visited the mall daily.

The mall did not have a big security budget, but the security supervisor did two particular things, largely theatrical, that basically stopped the drug dealers in about a week. First, he reached out to the local police department and told them they were going to set up an outpost for them where they could write reports or eat lunch. He also told the officers that if they chose to eat in the food court, they would be given priority when there were lines, as well as a discount. Now this is nothing new— lots of malls have police outposts and give discounts to officers. What this security supervisor asked that was different was, rather than have the police enter from the outside door of the outpost, they would enter from some other location so they would have to walk through the mall to get to the post. The department was pleased to do as the supervisor requested. Now the mall had a constant influx of police officers in uniform walking around the mall, and the mall didn't have to budget any money for the enhanced security presence.

The second and very sneaky thing the security supervisor did was request the police target the drug dealers by, once a month, bringing their drug dogs into the mall and spending some time walking around or even doing demonstrations from time to time. Great, right? Well, the supervisor also owned a Labrador retriever, so he had a vest made for the dog that closely resembled the vest worn by the police department's drug dogs. Several days a week the supervisor would simply wear a suit and bring his dog to work with him, keeping him on a leash as he went about his duties. Pure security theatrics, but in this case, it worked.

The difference between theatrics and smoke and mirrors that we discussed in Chapter 2 is that smoke and mirrors are made up of real assets that can actually work. They are just deployed in hopes that the bad guy sees them and is intimidated enough to walk away. Theatrics are an act and have no real value in defense. Rarely can you mix effective solutions and theatrics (as was the case with the security supervisor's Labrador) and get anything effective as an outcome. Theatrics are empty hope that actually put you in more danger, and even with the scenario in the mall, if the police presence wasn't common, the Labrador trick would eventually fail.

Pakistan Marriott Attack—Ineffective Threat Assessments

In contrast to the lack of understanding of attack possibility versus attack probability pointed out in the previous case studies are the attacks on the Marriott Hotel in Islamabad, Pakistan, in 2008 and the Boston Marathon bombing in 2013.

Because of its location near government buildings, diplomatic missions, embassies, and high commissions, the prestigious Marriott Hotel in Islamabad was under a constant heightened threat level and had a high attack probability. In response, Marriott took major precautions to thwart any number of terrorist attacks. As such, two major things occurred because of this prestige: patrons began to believe the possibility of a terrorist attack happening when they were at the hotel was low, assuming their security was taken care of, and simultaneously, terrorists became fixated on that location as a candidate for a grand attack.

After thorough surveillance, terrorists planned and successfully carried out an attack on the Marriott, where over 50 people were killed and over 200 injured. This particular hotel was heavily secured with numerous security guards, CCTV cameras, and fortified gates to prevent vehicle-borne improvised explosive devices (VBIEDs) from entering and attacking the hotel compound.

Why, with all these state-of-the-art security measures, were the terrorists still able to kill and injure so many? They simply built a bigger bomb. When analyzing this particular attack, it is quite evident that although Marriott security measures were somewhat up to date to prevent attacks within the compound, and even though they understood the attack probability and the heightened possibility of attack, the hotel's security threat assessments did not take into account an adequate standoff distance to defend against a very large VBIED. Their CCTV system did little more than record the attack; it was not set up to locate and record surveillance prior to the attack, or view the avenues of approach that an attacker might take. The cameras were simply pointed at the entrance as if they were focused on catching a robbery suspect. Regardless of all these preventable mistakes, the biggest contributing factor to the high loss of life and injury was the low awareness of the staff and individuals who normally stayed in the hotel or attended events there regularly and the inability of the hotel to forward-think the most likely attack while depending on defensive theatrics that were performed because "that's the way it's always been done."

The type of theatrics described by Pat in his video on range theatrics had more to do with techniques we are trained to do because of institutional inbreeding, taught because "it's just the way it is done," or perhaps they were techniques invented by someone who didn't really know what they were talking about in the first place. I see these theatrics constantly in professionals and individuals attempting to appear high-speed and secure. Yet as we continually show in most of the case studies, attackers, thieves, pedophiles, robbers, burglars, bullies, and basically anyone experienced in nefarious tactics can usually see directly through all of these theatrics and are in no way deterred by them.

So, as you build your defenses remember this: if it doesn't mitigate a vulnerability, help you develop a contingency plan, or guide you away from being caught up in a critical area, then it is most likely useless defensive theatrics, and it can make a problem worse.

CHAPTER 7

Defensive Actions

Defensive Aggression

"Violence of action" is a term most people associate with aggressive offensive actions taken by forces tasked with taking down an armed target. Military special forces units, SWAT teams, and even firefighters use violence of action to enter a situation with controlled aggression and overwhelming tactics and firepower. However, talk to an F-18 pilot guarding a U.S. Navy carrier strike force and you will see the same mindset and aggressive posture as the fighter pilot that is screaming toward an air-to-ground target such as an enemy headquarters they are going to bomb. Now I know it's a far reach from the mission of a fighter pilot to that of a parent taking their daughter to the latest teen idol concert. I mean, why would you ever need to be aggressive at something like an Ariana Grande concert, right?

On May 22, 2017, an Islamic attacker detonated an improvised explosive device (IED) outside of an Ariana Grande concert in Manchester, England, at the conclusion of the show. Just as I had predicted as a security specialist in 2003, again as an FBI Special Agent, and then on national television networks like Fox News and CNN almost two years prior, the end of concerts and other stadium-sized events are perhaps the biggest soft targets waiting to be attacked. As the Manchester attack showed, even a small IED packed with pieces of metal can kill a lot of people if the crowd is condensed and the security is weak. On May 22, twenty-two concertgoers (many young children) and their parents were killed just outside what would be considered the heightened security area located inside the arena. Two hundred fifty people were injured, some critically, with many of the injured being left with lifelong physical and mental issues.

I know this is a harsh statement, but I must point out that all these injuries and deaths were not a result of a terror attack; they were the result of a failure of every victim and their parents to secure their lives by developing knowledge and understanding of the changing history of Islamic attackers and the areas they were most recently targeting. Had the parents and to some extent the young people realized how easy it is to identify a soft target area, they could have combined that knowledge and understanding and realized they were walking into a critical area at a critical time. It should also be noted that this was a successful attack by an individual who went to great lengths to plan his attack, and most likely used some sort of target package he created or was given by an associate. This is why your defenses should be aggressively planned and aggressively carried out.

As we typically see, however, overall awareness at such events is practically nonexistent, as the rush of the atmosphere and electricity of the event overcomes most people's enthusiasm to watch out for bad guys. At a professional football game I attended for a threat assessment, my partner and I told the local police department and stadium managers that we would monitor the behaviors of the staff and patrons, then give them a detailed attack plan on how we could kill a minimum of 1,000 people.

Our mitigating factors for the attack plan were that the entire stadium staff had been trained in awareness, and millions of dollars had been spent on barriers that surrounded the stadium. These barriers were large steel posts about one foot wide and six feet long, with three feet of the steel posts buried and cemented into the ground and three feet rising into the air. The barriers were placed about two feet apart all the way around the entire stadium and were stable enough to stop a very large VBIED or, as we've seen lately, just a vehicle that is targeting people to run over.

By far this was one of the most secure stadiums we had seen. Every bag was searched, every person was scanned, and police presence was everywhere. Even police snipers were located on the roof of the stadium. This was not just security theatrics, and even more impressive was the fact that this was just a normal game.

However, the aggressive nature of the stadium security was just a sign that my partner and I, both Navy SEALs trained in unconventional warfare, needed to look for another critical area that we could attack, still affect the professional sport, and kill 1,000 people. How did we find this danger zone? We waited for everyone to leave and we looked left, where a busy five-lane road that ran between the stadium and the parking lot was located. Unfortunately, the aggressive defenses of the stadium were not matched by the same aggressive understanding of the city mayor, who refused to have the road shut down during major stadium events.

As 70,000 people exited the stadium, most made their way to that gigantic parking lot and, to our amazement, when the light turned green and the "do not walk" sign lit up, the police officers on the corner stopped the pedestrian traffic and let the vehicle traffic proceed. At one point, we counted over ten trucks with the same cargo capacity as the vehicle Timothy McVeigh packed with 5,000 pounds of ammonium nitrate explosives that he used to attack the Alfred P. Murrah Federal Building in downtown Oklahoma City on April 19, 1995.

A lack of aggression incorporated with threat assessments can often lead to these shared threats being overlooked. Shared threats are critical areas that can be exploited by a bad guy to attack the same people you are trying to protect. They are the least understood vulnerabilities to people and facilities when considering defenses and, as we see in the case of the stadium parking lot, a shared threat can be more of an enticing prospect than the actual hardened target nearby.

Studying the images of the neighborhood around the location of the VBIED that Timothy McVeigh detonated at the Murrah Federal Building, you can see that not only was the federal building destroyed, but 324 buildings within a sixteen-block radius were also destroyed or severely damaged even though they were not the actual target. This particular attack also killed 168 people and injured more than 680 others, many of whom were not visiting the actual target. It is safe to say that the surrounding venues did not understand an attack on the federal building would greatly affect their facility or kill their patrons. Unfortunately, after the fact, it became very evident that a shared threat can, possibly, end your life or destroy your business even if you are not the target.

Understanding this shared threat potential, it is also important to note that most of the site surveys done on a high-value target by state and local government security officials offer nothing to the surrounding facilities. Likewise, these site surveys do little to educate the general public on what to be aware of and how to react if an incident happens. This lack of dissemination of even basic information to the public is another example of the unprofessional and harsh reality we live in. Security and law-enforcement professionals often fail to understand that the main reason they do what they do is to keep people safe and alive. Yet those very people are not just left out of the loop, they are disregarded completely.

Comparing the widespread damage to the locations around the federal building in Oklahoma, imagine how many people would be killed if the same type and size of VBIED were driven up to the intersection between that particular stadium and its parking lot as the majority of 70,000 attendees of a professional football game crossed the road. It would be a national tragedy to say the least and quite possibly the largest loss of life at one time in U.S. history.

Needless to say, it was an eye-opener for that city, and a good example of not only how attackers think, but also how easy it is to invite an attacker to their target because you were not being aggressive enough in your threat assessments and subsequent defensive measures.

Controlled aggression is your friend when it comes to defending yourself, your loved ones, the facility you secure, the neighborhood you patrol, and the city, state, or country you manage. When I have been tasked with protecting someone or something when deadly force has been allowed, as a SEAL or law-enforcement officer, I knew that I could kill an attacker just as fast with a smile on my face as I could with a scowl. Aggression is not a look, it is an attitude. If you realize this and implement aggression into your defensive protective measure, you will identify ways to get around budgets, invent new ideas to replace old, useless tactics, and realize that awareness backed with effective targeting can defeat any attacker.

Defensive Participation

It is always important to include everyone in the defensive process, especially when you are going on vacation, on a field trip, or maybe just to work. If you apply the techniques of Attack and Defend by building an attack package on the area you are concerned with, discovering your critical areas, critical times, vulnerabilities, and avenues of approach for an attacker, you should share your new awareness with as many people as possible.

I often find that people are unwilling to put themselves or their reputation out there for people to criticize, especially when it comes to awareness discovery and what needs to be secured. I have talked to staff members at hotels who had a realistic awareness of threats in and around the hotel but were too intimidated by snotty management to share what they saw or offer suggestions. This is very unfortunate because it is often individuals who work in specific areas of a facility that have a true understanding of threats and best defensive practices in their area. To put it bluntly, security managers know paperwork and facility staff knows the reality of what's going on in and around the property.

The Boston Marathon Bombing

On April 15, 2013, in Boston, Massachusetts, two terrorists placed improvised explosive devices (IEDs) inside backpacks and placed them in the highly congested area around the finish line of the famed Boston Marathon. Although the finish line of a major marathon is known for its large, congested turnouts, the city of Boston chose not to restrict that area to ticketed patrons only, nor were there any screenings done of spectators and their bags. Even worse, the terrorists laid their backpacks on the ground in the middle of the crowd and walked away without anyone stopping them. In fact, the backpacks remained on the ground for over two minutes. One of the victims that helped identify the terrorists after having his legs blown off stated that he saw them set the bags down and walk away, yet he never gave it a second thought.

In all the preceding case studies, lack of awareness was the single biggest contributor to the attacks—by the citizens, unaware of possible threats, and by the authorities, unaware of massive gaps in their threat assessments. The result was a completely reactive response after the damage was done. Are you starting to see a pattern here? Attackers understand patterns of unawareness, and they use them to their advantage.

One year a bad guy can perform a dry run by carrying a backpack full of books into a restricted zone. If nothing happens, they may become fixated on breaching that vulnerability and exploiting it for attack purposes. As a civilian, you should never assume your safety is taken care of by external forces. As authorities, you should never assume putting on a good display of awareness will be all it takes to scare off an attacker. As an attacker, I see these vulnerabilities as giant gifts, waiting for me to utilize for an attack.

As I discussed in Chapter 3, attacks at special events in Israel rarely happen, because of the awareness level of officials and civilians at any given time. From the military to the straphangers on the local buses, awareness in Israel is a part of life. If a bus approaches a bus stop and a car is parked too close in a suspicious manner, everyone on that bus will be aware and most likely the bus will not stop. If I am an attacker and I see that level of awareness, I am more likely to skip that attempted attack because chances are I would be spotted doing surveillance and never even make it to the attack phase of the target package.

These same types of mistakes in defensive participation are often made with friends as they go on vacation or out for an evening of fun. One person has developed an understanding of where the danger exists but is either unable or unwilling to tell others in the group. In this case, it is the opposite problem from the staff that can't communicate with the manager—it is the group that is uninterested in hearing from the enlightened person.

In both cases, a lack of participation in the overall attack awareness is a key vulnerability attackers will prey upon. Drinks getting drugged in a bar, burglary in a hotel—it all can be greatly affected by a team effort, because every set of eyeballs is basically a sophisticated abnormal behavior radar system. Nothing can defeat an attacker better than an aware human, and a collective group of aware humans is the best defense system in existence.

Teamwork: Cleo and Friends in the British Virgin Islands

Take, for instance, my friend Cleo and her story that demonstrates the true effectiveness of the proactive targeting skills taught in *Sheep No More*. Cleo was going to take a trip to the Virgin Islands with two of her girlfriends. I knew she was going, so I asked her to read the draft version of this book, which at the time had not been completed. Her first comments after reading the draft was that the writing was good, but it seemed to be a bit repetitive. I explained to her that the repetitiveness was built into the book so that the reader could literally memorize the techniques while they were reading about them.

I learned this technique when I was figuring out how to study properly in Navy Officer Candidate School. Another officer candidate and I would walk in circles in the room while we repeated the key terms and definitions we would be tested on. As we walked in the circle and repeated the terms and phrases, we began to break them down to one or two words that we had to remember. When it was time to take the multiple-choice test, we literally didn't even have to look at the questions. We could simply look at the answers and if we saw the key words, and the rest of the answer made sense, we knew it was the correct answer. Likewise, the repetitive nature of the methods in this book is intentional so that you can flip the switch from attacker to defender in the blink of an eye.

Before leaving on her trip, Cleo sat down and did some quick remote surveillance of the area where she and her friends would be traveling. This computer surveillance included a quick map study of the resort where they would be staying, local demographics and crime statistics, taxi services, size of police force, and distance from the hotel to shopping and tourist locations. As she scanned through the online information, Cleo remembered not to look at her information from a defensive mindset but to continually focus on information collection for the purpose of targeting young, female, American tourists like her and her friends.

One of the biggest things she realized while doing this remote surveillance was that she and her friends were actually staying on the British Virgin Islands, not the U.S. Virgin Islands. Cleo did not make the reservations for the trip—that was handled by one of the friends—so this changed her perception of vulnerabilities that could be exploited by an attacker. Because the group consisted of all American citizens, they would have to work through the U.S. embassy if anything happened, which meant slower response times than if a crime were committed on U.S. soil. Also, their accents would be different, and that would make them identifiable as tourists, even if they attempted to blend in. When Cleo logged onto the U.S. State Department website and typed in "British Virgin Islands (BVI) travel advisory" she was comforted that there was no official advisory or warning of issues or threats. However, she was surprised to find the following warning:

Crimes, including murder, rape, armed robbery, petty street crime, automobile break-ins and burglary, do occur. Avoid walking alone, especially in isolated locations and at night. Do not leave valuables unattended in public areas, unsecured hotel rooms or in rental homes.

Seeing this, Cleo got to work looking for areas where young, female tourists would be most vulnerable to attack. It was at this point that she realized if she were going to attack herself and her group, the easiest place would be outside the hotel, possibly in a bar or between bars. This could include putting any number of drugs into their drinks, or simply waiting to see who would be the most intoxicated and following them. Cleo also noticed that the trip to and from the restaurants and bars was a considerable distance from the hotel, which included a long stretch of road where there was nothing—no other shops, restaurants, or hotels that might offer refuge in an emergency. This didn't really bother her because she figured if she were going to attack someone, it would be hard to confront a moving taxi.

This is an important side note, because as you will see, Cleo's lack of experience thinking like an attacker led her to overlook the danger of that dark and lonely area between the bars and hotel. In fact, she became so focused on what she thought was the most likely critical areas and avenues of approach for attack that she simply dismissed the possibility of other types of attacks. This is a common mistake for even the most seasoned threat assessors because the human tendency to say, "Ahh, nothing will happen there," is always floating in the fog of targeting. Like the fog of war, targeting can become so tedious that simple things can be overlooked, and once you go down that rabbit hole, it's as if a mental block is erected to keep you from seeing a particular area or time as critical.

After printing the information for herself and her friends, Cleo simply applied the Attack and Defend technique of thinking about why, where, when, and how attackers might target them in that area. The scenarios she contemplated were quite predictable and included their room being burglarized, being robbed when outside the hotel compound, spiked drinks leading to robbery or rape, petty thieves stealing purses and credit cards, and getting too drunk in an unfamiliar area.

Although there were several more scenarios she came up with, her new understanding of targeting paid off primarily in two ways. First, she flipped the switch from attacker to defender before she left. She gave the printouts to each girl going on the trip and had a short discussion about where they would be the most vulnerable, the times that increased their vulnerabilities, and how an attacker might exploit these vulnerabilities. She also pointed out the avenues of approach to her friends that an attacker might take and how it differed from a bar setting to waiting on the street for a cab. Sometimes the best avenue of approach for an attacker is approaching from the front and engaging the victim in conversation. Sometimes it will be from behind, where an attacker can grab a purse and run. And sometimes it's a standoff distance, waiting and watching for the opportunity to approach from any angle.

So, the girls set off on their weeklong vacation to the British Virgin Islands. Everything for the most part was very relaxed, and the times they spent away from the hotel compound were relatively uneventful, yet the girls did discuss the tactics of attackers throughout the trip. The seed of awareness had been planted! They made sure not to wear flashy jewelry. They did not use their cell phones when they were moving from location to location. And they all kept eyes on each other's behavior to look for the telltale signs of a spiked drink.

Then, on their last night out in town, the girls got into a taxi and asked the driver to take them to their hotel. This was a situation they had not planned for when they first arrived on the island, but as you will see, the technique of flipping the switch from attacker to defender had allowed them to quickly identify the long cab ride to and from the bars as a vulnerability even though they were seemingly safe in a taxi. This identification of a previously undetected critical area and critical time helped them set up actions that they would take if something happened, and it was a good thing, because the clock was ticking on their real-world test.

As the taxi traveled that dark stretch of road back to the hotel at about 2:00 a.m., they quickly realized something was not normal when the driver pulled over and stopped the cab on a lonely part of the trip back to the hotel. Immediately, all three girls had their cell phones ready. One of Cleo's friends took the lead in talking to the driver, while the other prepared to call the police (which all three had preprogrammed into their phones) and Cleo called the hotel. As the cab driver became agitated, he exited the vehicle. The girls, remaining calm, locked the doors. At that moment one girl was controlling the conversation with the cab driver, the second was on the phone with the hotel, and the third had already called the police, which they told the cab driver.

The hotel asked Cleo to confirm who the driver of the cab was; she did, and they knew him. They said that he was probably trying to figure out which of the two hotels this particular company owned on the island where the girls were staying. Cleo relayed this to her friend talking to the cab driver and told him which hotel to go to.

The agitated driver got back into the car and began to drive. Meanwhile, Cleo remained on the phone with the hotel and the third girl remained on the phone with the police, telling them where they were. As they got to the hotel, all three girls exited the cab and gave the money for the driver to the bellman. They felt that further contact with the driver would not be necessary, and that was probably correct. In the end, everything ended well, but no one knows why the driver actually stopped and began ranting in the middle of nowhere. Even the hotel staff could not explain why he would have reacted the way he did.

After Cleo returned home, I asked her what they were thinking when this unfolded. She told me that after their second trip to the bars, all of the girls agreed that the cab ride was their most critical area and late at night was the most critical time. However, they also realized that there was no way to avoid taking a cab to get home. That vulnerability stood out in their minds because they kept asking themselves subconsciously, *If an attacker was going to strike, how, when, and where would that be, and how can we mitigate these criticalities?* Now Cleo and her friends were seeing firsthand how quickly a person can broaden their understanding of attacks by simply playing the "what if" game and going back and forth from attacker to defender mindset. By the evening of day two of their trip, they had devised a plan of how an attack could unfold on their way back to the hotel in a cab. Then they predetermined standards of behavior so they could recognize if any of them started acting abnormal. They decided not to drink too heavily and they agreed on who would do what if an incident did happen, like who would call for help and who would stay focused on what was happening so someone could think clearly without distraction. They figured if an attacker knew they were on the phone with the police, they would be less likely to carry out an attack, and if they called the hotel, they would be able to further assist and direct them if it was a real emergency.

Had the girls blindly walked into that cab, their ability to react quickly and with calm calculation would not have been possible. Most of the time, when someone is caught in a scary, unpredictable situation, fear sets in and paralyzes them, or even worse, total unawareness of the danger may actually allow the attacker to strike with no defenses to stop them.

Because we don't know the real motivation for the cab driver's unexpected stop, we must assume the worst—that he was planning on some type of criminal activity, possibly even violent crime. Not all critical areas and critical times can be avoided in life, but they can be identified and mitigated. As in most unpredictable situations, there actually is some level of predictability if the proper mindset and targeting techniques are applied, which the girls proved in the British Virgin Islands. By being proactive in their trip planning, researching the areas in which they would be traveling, and understanding the techniques to identify vulnerabilities, Cleo and her two friends were able to proactively handle the danger that existed within one of their critical areas at the predicted critical time.

PART 4

ESCAPE, EVADE, FIGHT, AND FEAR

As I have been explaining all through this book, proper attack planning starts with knowledge, seeks understanding, and makes the effort to gain experience so that you know what will actually work and what won't when it comes to defending yourself, your family, or even your homeland. This process is exactly what the technique of Attack and Defend is about, and if you ever find yourself in the unfortunate position of dealing with an actual attack, you will have to deal with three major factors:

- *Fear*, which limits your actions and clarity of thought.
- *Action*, which is the result of preparation, training, knowledge, understanding, and experience.
- *Reaction*, which is based on an assumption of what you know in that second of time.

As we traveled through the preceding chapters, take into account that we transitioned from the mind of an attacker in order to learn what they will target to the mind of the defender in order to set up proper defenses based on who will attack, why they would attack, and where, when, and how they attack. You have heard the terms critical areas, critical times, vulnerabilities, and avenues of approach so many times that you will probably dream about them and their significance.

But now it is time to transition into the mindset you will have when you actually find yourself in a situation. Putting things down on paper is equivalent to gaining the knowledge and understanding needed to prepare your defenses and SOPs, but you must have experiences. Believe it or not, reading case studies and envisioning yourself as the target or victim will in fact help you develop this mindset, and it will also help you understand what you have learned.

If you have ever seen the Jimmy Stewart movie *It's a Wonderful Life*, you will see a similar circumstance where the main character is taken by his guardian angel to see all the people he has unknowingly helped and in turn it helps him. While not exactly the same concept, you can actually gain understanding about effective tactics by reading what worked and what didn't work for others in times of crisis. Another way to look at it is as if case studies are simulators that allow you to practice your new awareness while introducing yourself to your own behaviors when they are pressed with fear and anxiety.

So, as you go through the last few chapters, put yourself in the shoes of those individuals you are reading about and apply your knowledge and understanding. Ask yourself what you would have done differently, if anything. And in all scenarios, see yourself as victorious.

If you enter into a bad situation thinking like a winner, chances are you will be a winner when it's all over.

CHAPTER 8

Escape

CONTRARY TO WHAT YOU have been taught your entire life, tough guys do run. As a Navy SEAL, the one thing we trained for more than anything was running. In Basic Underwater Demolition SEAL (BUD/S) Training, students run an average of nine to thirteen miles per day. Of course, that is mainly to ensure our bodies and minds are taken to a limit most would think is not humanly possible, but while we are being broken mentally, we are also being conditioned for the fog of war.

The SEALs are a small, unconventional force, often used in battle against much larger forces. Therefore, we must be in good enough shape to perform fast and aggressive in a dirty and dangerous environment. But we must also know when to break contact with an enemy and depart a target area when the mission is accomplished or when we are faced with a situation we are not going to overcome with the resources we are able to present.

Knowing when to run is very important when you are caught up in a fluid situation, especially if bullets are flying. Sometimes you will be better off walking at a brisk pace, and other times you will be best crawling out of the danger zone. For example, if you are in a facility and you hear gunfire, you must assess the situation before running for several reasons. Sound travels in ways that can be highly unpredictable—it can be influenced by the shape of the walls, floors, and ceilings, and it can appear to be behind you when in fact it is coming from a direction directly in front of you. You may perceive sound differently than the person standing three feet away from you. If a gunshot rings out and an individual across the room screams "Run!" and takes off to the left and you follow, you could be reacting to someone who has heard a bent or reflected sound wave. Yes, I know this is difficult to comprehend when you are hearing gunshots, and you're sitting there reading this thinking, *If I hear shooting, I doubt I will be in the position to do a full spectrum analysis of the sound.* I know, I get it, but it is very important you at least understand that these are the variables you could be faced with when you find yourself in a violent encounter.

Once you determine where the sound is occurring, or maybe you have a visual of the actual attack, it may still not be time for you to run right away. You need to keep thinking about an *effective* escape that doesn't lead you to more trouble. There have been numerous attacks on record where multiple attackers approached from various avenues of approach and people ended up running right into another attacker because they did not assess the situation before they ran. I recall watching the attack on police officers in Dallas, Texas, on July 7, 2016, by a terrorist named Micah Xavier Johnson, during a protest march of about

800 people, and being guarded by 100 Dallas police officers. As the attack unfolded, some of which was recorded, Johnson moved on the ground picking out targets as officers ran toward the sound of the shooting.

Although this is a standard operating procedure for active-shooter response by most law-enforcement agencies, they have failed to add into the equation the proven tactic of capturing a high ground for overwatch. Had Dallas PD placed an officer on top of parking garages or in buildings along the protesters' route, the possibility of an officer being able to kill the shooter would have been much higher than trying to engage him by simply running toward the sound of the shooting.

While there is a considerable difference between a civilian trying to escape from a violent act and a police officer engaging a shooter, the premise is the same. Analyze the situation before you make the decision to move. If you don't, you could be running into an attacker's crosshairs. However, if you get frozen and over-analyze the situation, you could similarly find yourself staring at the attacker because you failed to make a decision. Remember, it has been proven time and time again, action beats reaction. Even with the most robust plan in place, you will need to make conscious decisions and actual movements when you are caught up in a dangerous and stressful situation. Don't get frozen!

This is where your understanding of cover versus concealment comes into play. Cover can both hide and protect you, while concealment typically only hides you but most likely will offer little protection. Despite what you see in the movies, most materials that walls are made out of will not even stop a handgun bullet, let alone a round from a shotgun or rifle.

So, you need to change your thinking that it is not just running but in fact it is *escaping* that you must concentrate on. One of the reasons I prefer the term "escape" versus "run" is that the attack you are faced with may not be an active shooter. For instance, vehicular attacks have become more and more common because they are relatively cheap and easy to carry out. Most of these types of attacks can be avoided by performing the Attack and Defend technique and determining the critical times for the critical areas you will be visiting and either avoiding it all together or determining the most likely avenue of approach and avoiding that.

On July 14, 2016, in Nice, France, just after 10:00 p.m. at the end of the Bastille Day celebration, a large cargo truck driven by an Islamic attacker plowed through the crowd killing eighty-six people along a 1.1-mile attack route. The attack lasted around five minutes and was initially possible because law enforcement had not properly blocked off the pavilion that was closed down to traffic for the celebration.

Similarly, on June 3, 2017, in London, England, a van, also driven by Islamic attackers, targeted pedestrians walking across London Bridge. When the van crashed shortly after the attack started, three male attackers exited the vehicle and ran to the Borough Market pub and restaurant area and started stabbing people. Eight people were killed and forty-eight injured. Of the eight fatalities, only three were killed by the rampaging vehicle, while five of the deceased had been stabbed to death.

Let's analyze these real-life scenarios and see how escape was possible. First and foremost, in the day and age that we live in, you must accept that bad people are going to continue to do these types of bad things. This does not mean you need to live in fear, stay at home, or freak out every time a vehicle drives by as you eat in a cafe or walk in a public area. On the contrary, as I have explained throughout this book, you have the ability to know just as much about the target area as the attacker. You can identify the most critical time for an attack, just like the attacker does. In both scenarios in France and England, the attackers chose very critical "soft" areas and times that were absolutely critical. They didn't carry out those attacks at 3:00 in the morning when no one was around. The attackers did their homework and determined that a celebration or a known tourist area where heavy foot traffic existed would be the perfect location for a simple vehicle attack and, in the case of the London Bridge attack, a follow-on stabbing rampage.

The tourists and patrons in England and spectators in France also knew this same information; they just looked at it in a different way. In Nice, people didn't go to the promenade at 3:00 a.m. to celebrate Bastille Day when no one was there. On the contrary, they did their research on the computer (just as the attackers probably did) and determined the date and time when all the fun stuff was going to be happening. Now if the bad guys can look at the same information as the celebrants and come up with an attack plan, the celebrants should also be able to look at that information and determine that the possibility of an attack is high, especially in Europe, and create their own attack plan to match the actual attacker's plan.

If the people or police had done this, the attack probably would never have been effective, and if the attackers had been able to get on the promenade, the people there would have possibly had a plan, choosing to sit or stand behind barriers if they existed, or simply avoiding getting caught up in the center of the crowd. They could have also derived a plan to run if a vehicle came barreling down the promenade. After looking at a map of the Nice attack scene, I am 100-percent confident that any individual who had considered the possibility of a vehicle attack would have had the wherewithal to stay close to the edge of the road and/or run horizontal to the road to either the beach or the buildings on the opposite side. Because I have studied these types of attacks, I am familiar with the typical reaction people have and, believe it or not, it is typical for a person to freeze, or run in the same direction as the vehicle is traveling without veering off to the side where cover may exist.

So, as you can see, running does not necessarily equal escaping the attack. I will continue to say it over and over: have a plan before you go, and see the area the way an attacker would see it. Most likely you will then make the correct decision if an attack occurs.

When we look at the London Bridge attack, most likely the people struck by the van were in the wrong place at the wrong time with little warning to react. From the limited video I have seen of the second stage of the attack, where the occupants of the vehicle got out and started stabbing people, it appears most people were caught so off guard that they paused to figure out what was happening. As a result of that brief pause, they were caught up in the offensive rush by the attackers and subsequently stabbed. Following the principle of developing awareness, if you have considered the possibility of an attack and envisioned what type of attack is most likely to occur in a given area, your ability to sense something is wrong most likely will be much quicker and in turn your actions will be much more structured and aggressive.

In the case of the London Bridge attacks, running away from the attack scene as fast as possible was the best course of action. But determining something was happening in the first place was actually more critical. The most important action (reaction for most people) was quickly determining they needed to run from the danger. The people who failed to act quickly suffered serious bodily injury or were killed.

Analyze the situation as quickly as possible, determine the nature of the threat and the threat direction, then escape from the scene accordingly. These are the steps to survival in a critical situation. Like everything else I've included in this book, if you consider these steps long before an attack happens, you will most likely survive by escaping the initial moments of the attack.

CHAPTER 9

Evade

CONSCIOUSLY HIDING IN AN attacker situation such as an active-shooter scenario is, basically, one step away from putting your destiny in the hands of the very person seeking to kill you. I've been interviewed on this subject numerous times on television and radio, and I always say I find it hard to believe how quickly living, intelligent creatures such as human beings will resign themselves to one possible choice for survival.

If you determine that hiding is your best option, remember that when choosing a hiding location, consider cover and concealment. Cover can offer some protection from bullets, even if it is only a locked room that will stall an intruder, while concealment is just another name for camouflage and offers little to no protection other than keeping you out of sight. Knowing this, you should see why we should focus on evading an attacker and not simply hiding.

While hiding can be a part of the equation of evading, you should always be ready to move, because almost 100-percent of the locations you will hide for the purpose of "sheltering in place" will provide little protection from a bullet shot from a high-powered rifle. A 7.62-millimeter round used in weapons such as an AK-47 can penetrate walls made out of cinderblock and continue straight into a person's torso with fatal results. With this understanding of ballistics in play, you should realize that wooden doors, drywall, plaster, and glass don't have any hope of providing you adequate cover in an active shooting incident, even if the shooter is only using a smaller caliber handgun. Unless you are enclosed in a bullet proof safe room you should assume that ballistic penetration is possible for whatever cover you can find as you will most likely not have an available ballistic rating labeled in or around your hiding space.

If the attacker is carrying out a knife attack, then the equation changes and if you can get yourself into a facility or room that can be locked and is not easily broken into, then that may be your best choice. However, I would recommend still keeping your options open for evasion leading to escape, regardless of what type of violent attack is happening.

On September 21, 2013, at the Westgate shopping mall in Nairobi, Kenya, multiple gunmen (at least four) entered the upscale mall and attacked using explosives, grenades, and AK-47s. Although details are a bit sketchy as to what exactly happened on the inside and how long the actual attack lasted, reports from U.S. officials stated that the majority of fatalities occurred within the first two hours of the attack. In all, 71 people were killed, including 4 of the attackers, and more than

175 people were wounded. The attack was carried out by the fundamentalist Islamic group al-Shabaab.

I was unable to find any information about individuals being killed as they attempted to flee the scene; however, I did see video of people trying their hardest to crawl into spaces too small for their entire body to hide and/or trying to hide behind something that did not actually conceal them at all. There were reports of some people hiding in stores on the second floor who were later rescued. Regardless, everyone who sustained a fatal wound sustained it inside the facility, not outside. So your goal in this type of an incident is to get out and away from the facility, especially in foreign countries where the responding authorities may be just as likely to shoot you as the bad guys or, as was the case with the Westgate mall, do some looting instead of rescuing anyone.

A few recurring themes jumped out at me in numerous active-shooter situations when people attempted to hide.

First, if you are lucky enough to find a place that completely conceals your body from the attackers, you may actually be stuck there for some time. As was the case in the Westgate mall, some people were inside the building for several days before being rescued. Now, I'm not telling you that you should leave a perfectly good hiding space, but I'm not sure how long is long enough. If you do not hear movement or gunshots for a prolonged period of time, movement should at least be considered. Furthermore, if you were to perform a proper analysis of the layout of the facility prior to spending time there, you may have a good picture in your mind (or, if you're smart, saved on your phone) of where the closest exit is located. If you are crammed into a space that doesn't allow you to move, a fast escape may not be possible because you have been in the same position for so long that your limbs are literally too cramped and stiff to run. I know this sounds a bit unlikely, but the person that considers all contingencies will be more likely prepared for the tiny hiccups that cause catastrophic results.

The second issue I have seen that constantly recurs in these active shooter or knife attacks is the useless tactic of falling on the ground. On January 6, 2017, at the Fort Lauderdale, Florida, airport, an active shooter killed five people and injured six; thirty-six others sustained injuries from the panic that ensued. The entire attack lasted only about a minute and twenty seconds before the shooter was taken into custody. In one video captured on security cameras near the baggage claim area, the shooter can be seen pulling the gun and shooting before he disappears out of the frame. What takes place behind him is not a scene of death but a scene of bewilderment and complete failure to act on the part of the civilians witnessing the shooting. Many people not only lay down, several literally jumped, spread eagle, onto the ground in the middle of the floor, possibly injuring themselves from the impact. Other people can be seen moving toward the only possible cover or concealment in the room, the conveyor mechanism. However, the conveyor belt is not what they hid behind. They chose a luggage cart made of small tubular metal that didn't offer either cover or concealment.

Now, what is even more alarming (besides the numerous people who just stood there without moving) is that I only saw one person move toward the door. Everyone else pushed inward toward the middle of the room. I have been to that airport as a federal air marshal and as a civilian traveling on business and I can tell you that from the conveyer belt area it is possible to exit the building in a matter of a few steps in some places, and in others it's merely a few fast strides. Yet only one person moved toward the door; the rest simply stood, crouched, or lay down, and a few apparently tried to fly. Yes, this is a bit of gallows humor, but what is not funny is that all of the people in that video were unable to act because they had no plan, and I can guarantee that none of them had done any type of a threat analysis that included a potential active shooter at the airport.

The next time you watch a video of people reacting to a terrorist incident after you have read this book, you will ask yourself, "What were they thinking?" Well, the answer is that they weren't. They were instinctually reacting to a fight or flight stimulus in their brain, with no training or understanding of how to survive.

If you've ever seen someone intoxicated or on drugs doing odd things, it is similar to someone reacting to high stress in that the brain is dealing with chemicals that have impaired the ability to think clearly. Adrenaline is a very powerful chemical and when it is combined with fear and surprise, you will see reactions similar to an individual who is impaired by a substance.

So, now you see that a task as simple as getting behind something to shield you or camouflage you from an attacker can be a mountain of a decision if you are not prepared. If you are not prepared, you will most likely be impaired. Imagine trying to then evade or escape from an attacker. You must prepare your mind, and so the hardest choice to make in an active violent situation is what we must discuss next—the fight!

CHAPTER 10

Fight

SEVERAL YEARS AGO I had two unique encounters in the green-room at Fox News while waiting to go on Sean Hannity's show. I had the good fortune of meeting heavyweight boxing legend Evander Holyfield on one occasion and mixed martial arts legend Chuck Liddell on another. The similarities were striking in that both men were profoundly confident, not really chatty, and really down to earth.

I did some boxing in college and I've been in a few fights throughout my life not associated with any type of sanctioned sport. As always, I am constantly analyzing different aspects of life as well as people's behaviors, and I can without a doubt tell you that when most people are confronted with the thought of fighting, it is more like watching the mating rituals of peacocks than it is people like Holyfield or Liddell in the ring. Most people don't want to fight, and in most fights that occur, the participants want the other person just to back down. It is nothing like when a skilled fighter is fighting another skilled fighter, where they have to go all in and commit to the fight. When normal people fight, the only commitment is usually the trash-talking and chest-pounding.

Let's take this analogy a step further. If a trained MMA fighter was at an ATM with his girlfriend when a stranger approached them with a gun and told them to give him their money, you can guarantee the reaction would be different than that of a person who has no training whatsoever. Although the MMA fighter may choose to hand over his wallet and not fight at all, the mere fact that he has experience in high-adrenaline decision making, along with experience dealing with someone who wants to hurt him, would greatly enhance his ability to remain emotionally stable and think clearly.

Now I am no psychic, but I can predict with some degree of educated analysis that a civilian who is not trained in the art of fighting, and in fact may not have ever been in a true fight in his or her life, will not react with the same level of emotional control and clear thinking. I have seen some of the biggest trash-talkers get knocked to the ground because they ran their mouths and truly believed that the other individual would relent. Pride often gets in the way of these boastful maneuvers, but imagine if this same snappy talker had a gun pulled on them by their opponent. In most cases you would see a complete turnaround in behavior because they know, intrinsically, that the battle has now shifted in favor of the opposition. They will also feel a burn in their gut so deeply that they will find it hard to breathe. If fear is not checked at that point, the person that was initially an Academy Award-winning trash-talker will be reduced to tears and legs so shaky it will be hard to stand.

I am in a unique position to discuss this experience because I have faced a gun as a young boy and as an FBI Special Agent. Once was as an innocent, untrained kid, the other as a seasoned unconventional warfare attacker, fully trained tactical defender, armed to the teeth and ready to fight.

Growing up very poor in the Ozark hills of northern Arkansas, I was raised with three sisters and no brothers. Needless to say, I developed a sense of humor very fast, as did the rest of my family. I was about ten years old and one of my oldest sister's friends was going to spend the night at our house. It was late, but she needed clothes for school the next day. My oldest sister is a bit older than I am, so she and her friend were accustomed to staying up and out later than I was. But they liked me (when they weren't the ones beating me up) and so they asked if I wanted to walk with them over to the friend's house to get the clothes. Of course, I said yes—it was summer in Arkansas so it was around 9:30 at night and about 94 degrees outside, just the way a kid likes it.

Long story short, when we arrived at my sister's friend's house, everyone was asleep. Considering this was Arkansas around 1979, the doors were unlocked. It was her house, and so we all quietly walked inside and went upstairs. As we climbed the stairs, my sister, with her sense of humor blazing, whispered, "Okay, let's go for the valuables first," and then giggled. When we got to the top of the stairs, there was a lounge chair against the wall facing the stairs so I sat down, as I wasn't interested in helping them pick out clothes for school.

As I sat there quietly minding my own business and thinking whatever a ten-year-old thinks, I looked up to see the business end of a .38-caliber revolver about two feet from my face. The friend's dad unfortunately had heard my sister's joke and evidently thought it was burglars going through the house, which was interesting because no one had been burglarized in that town in my lifetime.

I deeply remember two things about that moment in time. I remember that I was completely frozen with fear, unable to move or speak. I literally had zero brain function—I just felt terror. However, to this day, more than thirty-seven years later, I can close my eyes and picture the size of the opening at the end of the barrel that was so profoundly staring at me like a steel monster, and I could somehow see the grooving pattern inside the barrel that snakes down to the chamber where it guides the bullet out of the gun.

I tried to explain to him who I was as he yelled at me, but I literally couldn't speak. That's when my sister and her friend heard the commotion and came out into the hallway. I sat there crying and shaking wondering if I was in trouble. How twisted is it that I grew up loving guns!

Well I did grow up and I do love guns and the God-given freedom the founding fathers of this great nation ensured was in our Constitution. It goes without saying that by the time I was living in New York as an FBI Special Agent on a criminal enterprise squad, I was very familiar with firearms of all sizes and calibers, and their specific uses. My tactical skills were honed from my years carrying them, training with them, and operationally employing them. The first time I strapped a gun on my side in an official capacity was in North Little Rock, Arkansas, at Camp Robinson National Guard base, where I was commissioned as a state police officer (*not* a "state trooper"). Camp Robinson was and is an outstanding department that patrols a

33,000-acre Army National Guard base, and it was a great place for me to start my career in service to the nation.

I remember wearing that gun for the first time and feeling proud, confident, and overcautious at the same time. The difference from that time in 1997 to 2009 was twelve years of the most difficult and challenging military training in the world, combined with shooting on a range every day at the Federal Law Enforcement Training Center (FLETC) in Artisa, New Mexico, where the temperature got as high as 114 degrees, and later at the FBI Academy in Quantico, Virginia, where your gun became your spouse.

The first day on the FBI range in 2005 our primary firearms instructor (awesome man) told us in a bold fashion that we would be shooting 3,000 rounds through our Glock 22s over the next eighteen weeks. Students literally looked at each other in amazement and some in fear, as they had never shot a gun before. I slowly looked at the student next to me and proclaimed that when I was a SEAL, we spent a month at John Shaw's Mid-South Institute of Self-Defense Shooting in Memphis, Tennessee, where we shot 3,000 rounds every *day* for a month. That is a good example of the level at which SEALs are trained to operate versus law enforcement.

The point of this long historical background is that in or around 2009, on another summer night, this time in the big city of New York, my squad had just ended a surveillance and everyone was heading back to the office. It was about 12:30 a.m. and we had been following a gang that was looking to do some damage to a rival group for reasons we won't discuss here. As I was sitting in my undercover Ford minivan in the turning lane at a stoplight, the vehicle in front of me went into reverse and moderately backed into me. The vehicle then ran the red light and made a left turn. Because I was an FBI Special Agent, my job was not to pull people over and issue traffic violations—that was beyond my authority. But I did watch as the car made a U-turn and quickly parked. Now it was facing me as I sat at the red light waiting to turn, and I monitored the two male occupants as they exited the vehicle. Just then my light turned green and I slowly turned left, not taking my eyes off the two individuals who were now on the sidewalk screaming at a third male. Individual number three took off running like a character out of the *Grand Theft Auto* video game, arms flailing, screaming, and that's when I noticed that one of the two occupants of the car had a gun. I could not see what the second individual that got out of the car had in his hands.

I called out my location over the radio and that I was watching an armed attack in progress. There was no response. *Damn these radios*, I thought. *Never working when I need them.* I called out again, no response. I later learned that for some unknown reason everyone had decided to just turn their radios off as they drove back to the office. Not something I would ever do, but that's not a tactical problem we are going to solve here.

Back to my dilemma. Directly in front of me, two male suspects (one with a gun) were chasing a third individual who was running like his pants were on fire and his legs had steel rods in them. As they neared the far corner across a large intersection, the two suspects tackled the third individual and started beating him. I slammed on the gas of my badass Ford minivan and was there so fast that I literally didn't have time to hit the lights. I had to make a split-second decision, so I chose to call out on the radio again. Still nothing. I slammed my van into park and jumped out, quickly drawing my awesome full-sized Glock 21 .45-caliber handgun.

Just a side note—when you draw a full-sized Glock 21 and enter a fight, the feeling is only comparable to the story of Samson in the Bible when he pulled out the jawbone of a donkey and killed a thousand men. It's a confident feeling!

I yelled, "show me your hands" as I trained my Glock on the individual I knew had a gun. I grabbed the second attacker by the back of the shirt and yanked him up with such force that he was leaning backwards toward me, so I kicked the back of both his knees in order to bring him down to a controllable position on his knees facing away from me. I moved my left hand back to my Glock, joining my right hand in a firm and steady grip, trigger finger pressing the slack out. I shoved the guy on his knees forward with my left foot, took a step back, and repeated my command: "Show me your hands and don't move!"

I now had both attackers in my sights and off the victim, who was curled up in a ball bleeding. The attacker who was face-down on the sidewalk was complying and had his hands spread out to his sides, but the individual who previously had the gun was not showing me his hands. He was about four feet away (about the same distance I was when I was ten years old with a .38 in my face). Once again, I yelled "show me your hands" and I might have added a few extra words in there at some point. Slowly he raised his hands, my eyes keyed in on his waist and both of his slow-moving palms. He was a trigger pull away from feeling the mighty force of a .45-caliber bullet, about the size of a well-fed bumblebee, placed right between his eyes. I was razor sharp in my focus, ready to kill this human being in front of me if I saw the slightest hint of gun metal in his hands or waistband. All my training at Camp Robinson, in the SEAL Teams, Federal Air Marshal Service, and the FBI had come down to this one moment, and I knew if he presented a weapon I would be fully justified to shoot him.

It was at that moment, when his hands were fully presented and his shirt had risen above his pants line as his arms went above his head, that I realized he didn't have a gun any longer. I stared at him as he stared at me and I said, "Get on the ground." He didn't. I said it again, but he just stared at me. Then as I looked so deeply into his eyes that I could see what he was thinking, I changed my mantra and said, "Don't you run," but it was too late. His mind was already turned and running, and so his body did the same thing.

Rather than get into a foot chase with no backup, I holstered my mighty Glock, picked up my fresh catch of bad guy, and because he then wanted to wrestle with me, I introduced his face to my friend Mr. Knee. He must have understood Mr. Knee because his response was to do as I said. An NYPD street crimes unit rolled up at that moment and helped me take him into custody. As they were patting him down, they pulled a screwdriver out of his pants that was about a foot long with a sharpened end. Even when you think you have everything under control, you find out you were possibly a second away from being shanked.

Now, with all that being said and those two stories in your mind, consider that most people in this world are trained about as much as I was at ten years old, paralyzed with fear as a gun whispered sweet nothings in my face. Most people, without training, will be just as surprised and unable to respond to an overwhelmingly stressful situation where the possibility of death is staring at them as well.

Add to that scary thought of being frozen by fear that the attacker systematically killing people will most likely be even more comfortable with the thought of taking a human life as I was as I held two bad guys at gunpoint. Although they will probably not have my level of training, their focus will be animalistic and void of compassion, which goes even beyond my mindset when I am tasked with potentially taking a life in defense of our country.

So, in order to fight a bad guy or anyone else for that matter, you have to show up on game day with some level of mental training at the very least. Hopefully that will also be combined with an understanding of who is attacking you, why they are attacking, and where, when, and how they are carrying out their attack. If you bring that to the fight, you may actually find yourself on the winning end of a confrontation where fighting your way out is the only option.

Lastly, as I have mentioned before, violence of action is a term often used by special operations units to describe their mental state, their aggressive actions, and their state of being. But you don't have to be a special forces warrior to harness the power of violence of action. When you are prepared for the fight, you will be able to show up to the fight with a clearer mind and a better understanding of all possibilities that could occur. And if you decide to fight, it is a commitment that has to be made now, not then. You have to sit and run some scenarios through your mind and commit to the fight.

If you were in the Borough Market area in London on June 3, 2017, when the stabbing commenced and could not run away, fighting would have been your only option. Consider this and ask yourself, are you going to commit to the fight? If you are a college professor and as you are lecturing you notice the door to your right opening and a student stepping inside, but instead of moving toward a desk, he drops a duffle bag on the floor and starts to unzip it. Are you going to wait to see if he has an apple for you or if he has a fully loaded shotgun capable of ripping your head completely off your shoulders? If you decide to make a physical move and pounce on him, are you just then in that moment going to make up your mind to fight? Understand that if that is the case, and you wait until that day to fight, your commitment will be greatly reduced to a reactive response and there is a good chance you will lose that fight. However, if you commit now and say to yourself, *I know my classroom well enough to realize a student coming in late and stopping at the door, dropping a duffle bag, and bending over to unzip it is a threatening maneuver. I am going to hit, tackle, stomp, bite, and gouge him until the threat is eliminated. I will move without worry or hesitation because I know I am right in my analysis.* If you rehearse that in your mind, chances are you will completely disrupt the crucial moments at the beginning of an attack and hopefully rally others to jump in and help. Remember, most mass shootings that are not terrorism-related last approximately three to seven minutes before law enforcement arrives to engage the shooter. However, during that short period of time, statistics show that most of the dead will be killed within the first 90 seconds. That's less time than it takes to order a meal at a fast-food restaurant, yet most people will dedicate more time and effort in determining what they will order for lunch each day than what they will do if the next 90 seconds determines whether they live or die.

Winning a fight takes approximately 25-percent mental preparation, 25-percent pre-committed will, and 50-percent technique. If you have either half of that equation, you are showing up to the fight with 50-percent more than the majority of humans that walk this planet.

So, fight as if your life depends on it, because in a violent attacker situation, it probably does!

CHAPTER 11

Fear Is Not a Gift

DESPITE WHAT SOME SECURITY "experts" may say, fear is not a gift. Fear is an emotion that's sole purpose is to make you fight or flee in times of great stress and danger. Unchecked, fear can literally freeze you in your tracks, crippling you from fight or flight. In certain cases, fear can cause you to make irrational decisions that result in situations just as bad as the original issue you were facing. Fear is the primary obstacle that you must overcome if you ever find yourself in an attack situation. Overcoming fear in a stressful situation is not something you just do, it is a skill you develop long before your day of reckoning is upon you.

Here is an exercise you can try if you're up for it. Fill a bowl or bucket halfway with ice, then top it off with cold water and let it sit for a few minutes so the water gets nice and cold. Take one of your hands and place it completely under the water and wait. You will reach a point where you have to choose either to bear extreme pain or to yank your hand out of the water. That is the point of fight or flight, and it can be a very scary time. Most people will flee, or in this case, immediately pull their hand out of the water when the pain of the cold starts to affect their nerves.

Now, here is a test. Take your other hand and do the same thing, but this time, make the commitment to sit for sixty seconds longer than you did before. For that sixty seconds, you have to try to focus on saying your multiplication tables out loud, i.e., "Two times one equals two, two times two equals four," and so on. If you can do this for just sixty seconds, you will experience a fraction of what it is like to make a decision when you find yourself in the middle of a fluid and scary situation. In essence, this exercise demonstrates the ultimate challenge of mind over matter in a stressful situation by mimicking the mental panic people face when fight-or-flight instincts kick in.

Now imagine if I knocked on your door and when you answered I took both your hands and forced them into the same bucket of ice water while I asked you a series of questions required to get free. Are you going to fight me to get your hands out? Are you going to stay calm and answer the questions to the best of your ability? Or are you going to just resign yourself to a temporary future of pain? Most likely you are going to fight to get your hands out or avoid the encounter altogether by foreseeing this and not answering the door. However, if it is unavoidable and you must answer the door, you should rehearse the experience several days before it happens so you can calmly carry out the tasks you are asked to do while in pain.

So, as you see, understanding fear and how you react in stressful situations will help you carry out actions in a more efficient and focused manner during times of duress. Also known as contingency plans, actions that you foresee then plan to deal with will help you visualize your actions so that you will be less likely to panic when it's time to act. Rehearsing these contingency plans will sharpen your reaction times and effectiveness as well as help you adapt in more fluid situations. That is what this book and the technique of Attack and Defend are all about.

As I wrote the scenarios in these next few chapters, I did not use a fictitious character name because I want you to see yourself as the character. Envision yourself as the person faced with this awareness situation and decides to come up with the plans of action. See yourself as someone who faces the consequences of not preparing. You see, there is a method to my madness. If I can get you to envision yourself in these situations, you will become more familiar with the technique of Attack and Defend as you produce your own target packages.

Consider fear as something that you can mitigate, just like a known threat to a specific target. Fear is your number one hurdle in times of crisis so as a defender, you must spend as much time as possible developing contingency plans that give you direction when predictable issues occur.

Imagine you have a fear of public speaking but you are set to give an important presentation at work. It is guaranteed you will feel anxiety and stress as you contemplate the mountain ahead of you. In order to control your fear, you have to face reality and develop a plan to act, not react. First thing you should do is devise an outline for the presentation. Next, you gather the equipment you will need and test it. Then you rehearse, over and over, until the verbiage is perfect, practicing breathing techniques and eliminating nervous fillers in your speech.

On game day, you arrive early, set up the equipment, and give your outline another thorough read-through. Once the audience convenes in front of you, you are fully prepared, which breeds confidence. You have tested your equipment and prepared backup handouts in case the equipment fails, mitigating all the different contingencies you could face during the speech. Because your preparation was so thorough, before you know it you are cruising to the conclusion without a glitch. That is how you control fear; that is acting, not reacting. You outline the situation, acquire what equipment you need, consider the criticalities, and then rehearse.

On the contrary, if you put off preparing for the speech because you are too busy or because you're afraid to face the fact that you're going to be speaking in front of a lot of people, game day will be 100-percent reaction. Chances are your equipment will have issues. You will have no backup plan, and your nerves will be so amped that you won't be able to breathe. You better hope your job is not counting on this presentation, because you have just demonstrated what happens when you fail to control your fear by setting up a completely reactive situation.

Now consider a different set of circumstances but with the same potential for preparation versus dropping the ball, and instead of losing your job, you could lose your life if you're not prepared.

In a month you are taking your family on a cruise to the Bahamas. It's been a long winter and for some reason spring is taking its sweet time to arrive. Every night you watch the news and like most people, you are aware of the spike in terror attacks around the world. Most of the attacks have been in areas outside the continental United States, although there have been several attacks inside the U.S. as well.

Even though you know there's a possibility that you and your family could be caught up in an attack on your trip, you decide that if it's your day to pay the man, you will be prepared as much as humanly possible.

Once you complete the target package outlined in this book, identifying who might attack you and your family and what their motivations could be, you begin to focus on applying your new attacker awareness. You make the shift by flipping the switch to the defender mode, coming up with as many different responses (contingency plans) to each possible attack you discovered in the critical areas and critical times you identified for the vacation.

One of the sectors that you consider as critical is the airports to and from your location. You learn from researching the history of recent terror attacks that airports are one of the newly preferred targets by attackers because of the routinely large crowds and the predicable vulnerabilities and unprotected avenues of approach. By looking at the tactics used in the numerous airport attacks, you notice that almost 100-percent of them were shootings that happened in and around the security checkpoint. Because you are a frequent traveler, you know exactly how the security check-points are laid out and each step you must take going through them.

So, using your defender hat to consider ways to mitigate your time in the critical area at the airport, you identify these critical areas to be between curbside drop-off at the departure area and the far side of the security checkpoint where you put your shoes and belts back on.

With that information, you devise the following steps at the conclusion of your target package, which you print out for your entire family to read.

Our Family's Tactical Airport Plan

Step 1—We all wear clothing that does not require a belt.

Step 2—Everyone wears shoes that are easy on/easy off.

Step 3—One family member will carry all the electronics and valuables (wallets, purses, and so on) in a carry-on. Cell phones stay with each individual.

Step 4—The person carrying the electronic items will be first in line so they can get through security with the important stuff if an issue arises. Also, this prevents our important and valuable belongings from being spread all over the conveyer belt. This point person will keep their phone with the other electronic gear, but every other person in the group will place their phone in their specific bin as they get ready to go through. The last person in the family line will keep their phone as long as possible until they are ready to go through the line. This will ensure that at least one phone is on either side of the security check-point as the family goes through. If the groups get split up, then communications can still be made.

Step 5—Everyone will keep their shoes on until they are all at the conveyer belt. When everyone is ready, they will take their shoes off and put them in one bin that person number two will control.

Step 6—One parent will be the first person through security and the other parent will be the last person through. [If you are a single-parent family, the adult goes last because you know through your research that the majority of people that have already passed through security will be able to escape an attack, so you want to send the kids through to the other side as soon as possible.]

Step 7—The area of commitment is the critical area where we are committed to move through security. Our shoes are off, our carry-on luggage is moving through, and we are waiting for the X-ray and/or pat-down. If a shooting happens when we are at this point, we will act with the same procedures. If part of the group is through security, they will run to Gate 22. [This is a predetermined area in the terminal you've identified and selected beforehand. It should not be too far away, but far enough that a stray bullet can't hit you.]

Step 8—During the attack, if something prevents you from getting through security to Gate 22, then you must assess the situation and run, opposite from the shooting if possible, to where we parked the car. [This is a location outside the terminal that's to be determined. Once you park the car, you send a text to everyone with the exact location so it doesn't need to be remembered under the tension of an emergency.]

Step 9—If you can't run, and cover or concealment is not available, grab anything you can use as a weapon, reassess the situation, and strike the attacker(s) if possible and as the opportunity arises (i.e., when the attacker reloads a weapon or turns their back to you).

Step 10—When the police respond, get ready to lie flat on the floor if they start shooting. If you are outside, and you have to lie down, remember that studies have shown lying in a depression in the ground 18 inches or deeper during a gun fight increases your survivability tremendously. Chances are that the attacker(s) will be standing along with the police so it is best to not be at their level, especially when the police respond with force. Lie low and flat and out of the way of the police.

Step 11—As soon as the attack is over, everyone should reach out to each other on their phones via the preset mass text. [Something you have already set up prior to departing for the airport.]

Although this feels a bit like overkill, your family reads through the steps and agrees to work together. Over the next month, you get the family together twice so that you all can rehearse your movements through the airports and how you all will react and follow the steps in case an incident occurs.

Now imagine, if you will, you and your family head to the airport on a hot summer day. It's humid outside and everyone is feeling uncomfortable and grumpy, but excited. This is the chaotic atmosphere when kids don't mind their parents and the people around you stop caring about other people's space.

You and your family arrive at the airport and park your car on level three, yellow zone. You send a mass text to the entire family so they will know what location everyone should head back to if an incident occurs and they get separated. After getting all your belongings together at the vehicle, you make sure that the point person going through the line first has all the electronics equipment (e.g., computers, iPads, and so forth) with them in a specific bag. While you check in at the ticket counter, you are aware (not paranoid) of any odd sights, sounds, or behaviors. Finally, you get your boarding passes and you all head to the security checkpoint. Now you're feeling kind of excited to see how this plan you have devised actually works out. You have put the checklist into your brain and you are walking through each step as they approach. So far so good—everyone moves quickly through the line because they wore no belt, they had slip-on shoes (which they all put in one bin), and the point person and all the electronics equipment has made it to the other side.

As the next family member is about to go through the X-ray machine, an agitated passenger behind you starts arguing with a Transportation Safety Administration (TSA) officer. The argument is over quickly, and the passenger calms down. As you scan back toward the X-ray machine, you notice that a piece of luggage is sitting by itself next to the extra plastic bins that you put your belongings in. You don't give it a second thought since there are a lot of people moving around.

You tell yourself that even though nothing is happening, you're glad that everyone is increasing their awareness through this exercise. And that is when it happens!

BANG!

Several loud bangs that you assume are gunshots ring out behind you from the left toward the ticket counter where you checked in earlier. In an instant, everything becomes completely chaotic. People scream as police officers come out of nowhere with their guns drawn, yelling "Get down!" while others are yelling "Run!" Your first inclination is to lie down and hide under the conveyer belt, but that's just because you've never been in this type of a situation before. It feels like it's been minutes, but it's only been fifteen seconds.

You know that three minutes is about the average time for a shooter to kill all their victims, and you know that the shooting is happening behind you, so you literally stand up, spread your hands out, and shove your family toward the opposite direction of the shooting. Because the family read and reread your Tactical Airport Plan and you all had rehearsed it twice, they immediately react to your direction, leaving their belongings on the conveyer belt and running.

The point person who was already through the other side of security had not had time to get her shoes on but already had all the electronics gear picked up from the conveyer belt after it went through the X-ray machine. The point person's eyes are keyed in on your reaction and literally says out loud "I'm going with them" and, rather than heading for Gate 22, starts running back through security toward the direction you all are running.

The point person made this decision because the sound was traveling down a hallway, making it seem as if the shooting were coming from the gate side of security. Remember, the fluidity of a situation can often cause issues you did not foresee, but if you have a plan of action, it is easier to adjust those actions than it is to invent reactions in the moment of chaos.

As the group is about to exit the terminal, a bomb goes off in the exact location you all had been standing in security. The force is so great that it blows all of you down and turns everything pitch black for about ten seconds. The bomb had been placed there a few seconds before the shooting started and was in fact the bag you had seen sitting by itself next to the plastic bins. An attacker was able to set it there, in the area where everyone was hurriedly moving, while a second person associated with the attack had a brief argument with the TSA officer.

As you gather your senses, you look up and see a light ahead of where you are now lying. You yell, "Everyone get up and run toward the light." Luckily your group is only shaken, but they are uninjured. However, the power of the blast disoriented everyone in your area, and your group is no longer moving together. Because you were able to keep your mind clear and yell out "run toward the light," everyone in your group starts moving toward the outside. Many people around you remain in the prone position on the ground, not because they are injured but because they are frozen with fear.

As you exit into the sunlight, you still hear the gunshots ringing out inside the terminal. You pause and start grabbing your family as they each emerge from the building. You all start running toward your vehicle, and because you mass texted it when you parked, you don't have to think about it; you just look at your phone and see "level three, yellow zone." You yell that location out loud several times while you assess everyone for injuries.

Finally, you and your family arrive at your vehicle and luckily your keys are in the bag with all the electronics gear that the point person didn't drop (having a second set of keys with the rear adult would be a great idea in case the point person got separated).

This attack is not over, so you have to decide whether to get in your car and drive off or wait and shelter in place where you are. What would you do at this point?

Now, the probability is very low that you will ever find yourself in an attack of this magnitude. However, the possibility is there, as attacks on airports are becoming more common simply because they are soft targets that have daily, predictable critical areas and critical times, vulnerabilities, and avenues of approach that never change.

With those facts in mind, imagine the outcome of that same situation if your family had no plan and just showed up at the airport ready for vacation. Chances are some, if not all, of your family would be dead or severely injured.

I have found that the most predictable influences on an individual's behavior in a fluid and scary situation are fear and chaos. Remember this mantra: "where chaos reigns, chaos rules." Reaction is always directed by emotion or at the least influenced by fear, both of which open a person up to chaos. Actions are directed by critical thinking and predetermined tactics, and this protects you from having a chaotic mind in a chaotic situation.

This may be difficult for some people to comprehend, but it is important for you to understand that you can have a clear mind in a chaotic situation. Have you ever seen a movie where stop action is being used? The actor stands and moves in real time while everything around them is moving in rapid speed. That is the way someone who has prepared themselves for action feels when they step into a chaotic situation.

"What should I do if I am caught up in a violent attack?" is probably the most asked question I get from individuals and during television and radio interviews. What people should be asking is, "What can I do now to prepare my mind and streamline my actions so I am fully aware so I may avoid attacks, and so that I am prepared to deal with fear and think my way through a violent attack if it cannot be avoided?" Hopefully, by this point in the book, that is what you are developing, as well as a much better understanding of who, why, where, when, and how most attacks could be carried out. Regardless, you could always find yourself in a bad situation under circumstances that may be unavoidable, such as attending classes, going out on the town, shopping, or just going to work.

Using the Attack and Defend system, you should be able to predetermine the critical areas, critical times, vulnerabilities, and avenues of approach for most attacks in the various aspects of your life. In the areas where avoidance may not be possible, you should have a plan of action that involves three options—escape, evade, or fight—or as we have come to know it, run, hide, or fight. Personally, I don't like the order of "run, hide, or fight" because people have begun to believe that hiding is a better option than fighting. As we have seen in most mass casualty terror attacks in recent history, almost everyone who ran lived, and many of the individuals who chose to fight back sustained injury and lived. The majority of deaths occurred when individuals tried to simply crouch behind an object or lay down on the floor.

As I have taught you throughout this book, understanding the mindset of someone who wants to attack you is the key to awareness of why, where, when, and how you could be attacked.

This understanding must be real, and you must commit to the realization that there are people that want to kill. They are not going to be talked out of it, or change their mind after they kill the first person. These people have resigned themselves to the lowest form of human existence in that they will purposely take the lives of other humans. They may be deranged, or they may be ideologues who actually believe they are doing you a favor by freeing your soul from sinful behavior. No matter why a killer sets out to attack, when a violent attack begins, your job is not to figure out how serious they are about killing, or how you may better understand their motivation. *Your job is to live!*

Remember what I said earlier: if you think like a winner, chances are you will be a winner when it's all over.

CHAPTER 12

A Final Warning

BEFORE WE MOVE TO the last section and final chapter, I want to share a warning that will in itself save your life. Lets reflect on the first two paragraphs in this book where I asked you to consider how much of your safety, your awareness, your health, your learning, your relationship with God, the safety of your children, your money, and so on, how much of all that and the rest of your life depends upon the protection of others?

Take your finances for instance. Do you rely on a money manager for your finances? If so, how closely do you monitor what they are doing with your money? How much do you know about the chances they are taking on your behalf? Do you know their education? Do you know their record for making people money from money? How much of other people's money have they lost in their career? When I was collecting information for *Sheep No More,* I asked a lot of people these same questions. I was astonished with how much of people's lives are blindly dependent on what they perceived to be the knowledge, understanding and experience of others, and how most people cannot see the reality of their own helplessness. I was truly shocked.

Today's world has become a training ground for learned helplessness. This frame of mind that lends itself to a dependent nature in all aspects of our lives is a manufactured state of being through rules, regulations, combined with a global cultural mindset of "I want it and you should get it for me." We are told to want, and convinced it's okay not to work for it, with desired recognition for having and little reward for earning. This is a cancer that can strike a free society where the people become self-indulged and comfortable as they drift away from a mindset of self-responsibility and personal awareness.

I live in Manhattan where it's not uncommon to see people yell at each other and get themselves into small fights here and there. One day when I was walking my dogs, I saw a guy in a suit, in or around his mid-40s, arguing with a group of teenagers from the local housing project (New York likes to put housing projects in proximity to high-income areas in Manhattan as a way to diversify.) Apparently, the argument began over the businessman's disapproval of fireworks the teenagers had been setting off in a little park adjacent to the apartments. The reason for the argument is actually not the focus of this story, but what is important is that as I saw the businessman pull out his cell phone and start videotaping the group of teenagers, the argument intensified. Suddenly the businessman turned and ran like an Olympic sprinter back into the building lobby with the group of teens hot on his heels.

As they entered the lobby, the doorman did his job and stopped the group from entering the building. Being the former law-enforcement officer that I am, my curiosity got the best of me and I quickly walked back inside to see the businessman yelling at the front desk worker to call the police. He just kept yelling, "Call the police now. Call them." His abrupt tone caught everyone standing in the lobby off guard, and that's when I looked at him and said, "You are holding a phone in your hand. What is stopping you from calling the police yourself?" For about 3 seconds everyone in the lobby stared at him in anticipation of the answer as he glared at me. So I asked again, "You have a phone. Why aren't you dialing 911?"

That's when he turned and walked away without saying another word. Since this is New York, no one thought about the incident longer than about ten seconds before going on with their lives, but I couldn't think of a better example of learned helplessness. Here was a full-grown adult human, capable of individual thought and reasoning, and with an instinctual desire for self-preservation. Yet he wanted someone else to take the initiative and call the police.

Now I am assuming the reasoning behind this decision, but based on thirteen years of living in Manhattan, working as an FBI agent, I can say I'm a pretty good judge of behavior motivation. I am convinced this individual did not simply dial 911 for two reasons; he didn't want to take responsibility for the actions that would require a police presence, and to be honest, I think he was so shaken up at one point that he forgot he had a phone. Regardless of his motivation not to dial 911, what was clear is that he had no plan to protect himself when he entered the argument, nor did he perceive the possible outcome of confronting the teens. He just did what his emotions told him to do, without any ownership of his own security, and so he fled to the safety of others and demanded that others work to protect him. That's learned helplessness.

This crippling state of mind exists in all aspects of life, and just like your new awareness of who, why, where, when, and how you can be attacked, sitting back and realizing how much of your life is relegated to dependency will shock you. When your freethinking is suppressed and individuality has deteriorated to a basic robotic state of being, you will automatically become increasingly dependent in every aspect of your life as well as more oblivious to where the threats of intrusion lie.

For instance, people turn all aspects of cyber security over to the newest technology to defeat hackers and trolls, yet they do nothing to modify their own behaviors of irresponsibility with password choices or policing what websites they are visiting into which they are inputting their own personal information. Online dating, for instance, is an area where people not only put their personal information, but they also thoughtlessly display an image of themselves for all to see without even a concern of the vulnerability they have created for themselves.

When I was in the FBI as a new agent, I was in the middle of my six-month rotation in the operations center of the New York office. As I sat there answering phone calls from complainants and emotionally disturbed people, I received a call from a woman that had inadvertently gotten herself into a situation that I guarantee could have been avoided if she had taken more precautions and researching the dangers associated with online dating before placing a profile online and blindly conversing with complete strangers. She had met a guy online through a dating application and struck up a relationship over text and phone conversations for about a month. As the two continued the long conversations and romantic flirting, they decided to meet when the guy would be visiting the U.S. in the near future to set up an orphanage, which he claimed was his career field, global outreach to orphans. Yes, that should have been the first clue that something was too good to be true; however, her expectation that people on dating sites were properly vetted led her to not research the typical scams associated with this type of social application.

Just before her love interest was to visit the U.S., he asked her for an odd favor. He said that because he was not an American citizen, he was having problems depositing and transferring money to build the orphanage, into an American-based bank. He asked her ever so politely if she would mind helping out the cause, by allowing him to transfer the money into her bank account, and when he arrived she could simply withdraw the money and donate it to the orphanage. Now despite the story of his background being too good to be true, and this strange request to transfer money, the woman agreed because she "felt like she knew who he was, and figured he was legit because they had met on a respected dating site."

The next day when she checked her bank account there was approximately one million dollars in her account. Luckily, despite her lack of self-responsibility and ownership of her own safety, a picture started to flash before her eyes that something was a bit over the top and that she should reach out to the authorities for guidance. I explained to her that she had made the right call, and that she was most likely being scammed. I instructed her to withdraw the amount of money she had in her account before the large deposit was made, and hold onto that money for the near future. I told her to then report the deposit to the bank and that the most likely reaction of the bank would be to freeze her account until everything was figured out, and even though that would be a hassle, the alternative would have been much worse.

Had she withdrawn the total sum of the fraudulent deposit and given it to Mr. Wonderful, he probably would have disappeared and she would have been responsible for the repayment of the balance of one million dollars back to the bank. Alternatively, had she not withdrawn her own money before filing a complaint with the bank, they would have most likely kept the full amount of her bank account, including her own hard-earned money. This lesson was unfortunately a harsh way for her to learn an important lesson about awareness and responsibility as the money deposited came from a fake bank from the region of Nigeria, which is known for these types of online scams using money orders backed by banks that exist in cyberspace only. In the end, her awakening came just in time to save her money and credit score. And trust me, the heart heals much quicker than the credit score.

To put the origins of this learned helplessness into perspective, consider the evolution of wolves into the domesticated canine. People who know me know that I love animals and my two dogs Rico and Jesse have consumed a large part of my life over the past seventeen years. Jesse unfortunately passed away in 2014, but Rico keeps on trucking even at such a remarkably old age. When we sit back and think about the reality of our canine companions, we should realize that they are the result of human interaction into their programming through selective breeding. At their core, dogs are instinctual hunters, encompassing the ability to seek out food, water, and companionship, as dogs are naturally pack-oriented. However, all of those instincts have been suppressed and/or modified through the years to create an almost completely dependent creature that fits our needs, and so we now have loving pets that truly depend on us to take care of their every need.

Similarly, this same process of learned helplessness has become the single greatest problem faced by mankind that closely mimics our canine friend's dilemma of reliance for life. The overall realms of society have become so dependent that the majority of the world's populations of human beings don't even know how to hunt or gather as we were born to do. In fact, if the electricity shuts off in a portion of even the most advanced cities around the world for more than three days, chaos will quickly ensue, and experts say that complete deterioration will take less than two weeks at the most.

The more aspects of daily life you incorporate into this awakening, the less likely you are to find yourself yelling for help in times of crisis like the businessman that cried out for others to act. Like everything else in this book, I truly believe that what I wrote and what you are reading was not just a coincidence. I wrote this book because I acknowledged a calling to help empower the world by sharing the techniques and skills of my expertise in targeting, which relies on awareness and an active understanding of the world you live in. You, in turn, are reading *Sheep No More* because you are called to the same state of mind of awareness and understanding. Your acknowledgement of a calling is in fact, an action, and in this case, it's an action that will propel you away from dependency.

Attack and Defend is more than just a series of steps for charting where you need to pay more attention to your daily

life. It is a technique that requires the readers to take ownership of their own protection. Ownership of your life is the same
technique of Attack and Defend, just on a larger scale, and it
is the foundation of awareness. As your mind expands into a
self-responsible state of being, it will open your eyes to successes
you never knew you were capable of and it will allow you to see
failures before they happen so you can prevent them from occurring in the first place.

Think of *Sheep No More* as the beginning of your awakening, not just a self-help book that helps you become more
secure. If you take the steps in this book seriously, not only will
you increase your awareness, avoid violent situations, and act
in a life-saving way if you encounter an attack, you will also be
taking a gigantic step forward in self-analysis and understanding
of what makes you tick and how much of your life you should
begin to take back from dependency.

Ultimately, we are the masters of our own domain, and,
whether we realize it or not, most of the responsibilities we
give away can be taken back with minimal physical effort. By
simply taking the time to dissect our lives into criticalities and
taking responsibility for our actions and owning the life we were
given, we can begin to make conscious choices that eliminate
surprise issues and increase our awareness, reversing the plague
of dependency. While I do not expect every human to become a
trained survivalist, I do hope that everyone who reads this book
will embrace the awakening it provides and in turn share their
knowledge of empowerment with everyone around them.

So, my final warning is this: dependency is the self-imposed
shroud that blocks awareness, and prevents action when action
is needed. Flee from dependency and take ownership of your life

and responsibility for your actions. When you do this, the true process of life and your ability to live it in a safe and productive manner will blossom.

PART 5

PUTTING IT ALL TOGETHER

An important part of the techniques in this book is the case studies of people, facilities, and cities that have been cited in many of the chapters. These are stories of individuals and facilities that have made strides in how they defend themselves simply by taking the time to evaluate their critical areas, critical times, vulnerabilities, and avenues of approach. In most cases, once a person or facility manager realizes that they have the knowledge and understanding an attacker is looking to gain and then exploit, their ability to discover true awareness and defenses increases exponentially.

As you will see in this last case study, newfound awareness can seem like a ball and chain that slows you down and dampens your fun. But as Susan discovered on her trip to the Philippines, her target package and the awareness it provided her eventually became her guide, not her burden.

CHAPTER 13

One Last Case Study

SUSAN IS A WELL-TRAVELED thirty-something-year-old who travels extensively with her husband. Together, she and Tom have nearly circled the globe because of Tom's job that allows them to take advantage of a high-level travelers' club. On one trip, they had traveled to Paris and were strolling on the Champs-Élysées, where she almost ran into a problem with gypsies who were known to work in groups to rob unsuspecting individuals, mainly tourists. Even after being told by hotel staff not to go out dressed in a provocative way, Susan did as she pleased and went out in the afternoon by herself dressed as if she was attending a fancy luncheon on Fifth Avenue in New York City. She hadn't even walked a block away from the hotel when she was approached by a normal, average-looking woman whose actions fit the description hotel staff had given her to watch out for. As the woman questioned her about where she was from and what she was wearing, Susan, based on the little bit of information she had learned from the hotel staff on how to react if approached, turned around and went quickly back to the hotel.

Susan realized at that time that she was wrong for casting aside important information given to her by hotel staff who knew what they were talking about. She realized the staff wasn't just telling her something they were instructed to say, but that they had seen the robberies and were trying to convey to her who, where, when, and how one of these robberies could occur and how she could avoid it. This encounter had a profound impact on Susan and how she would travel from that point forward.

Fast-forward another year, when Susan was watching TV and there was breaking news about a shooting at an airport. By coincidence, my bearded face was the one on screen talking about the importance of awareness and forward-thinking critical areas, critical times, vulnerabilities, and avenues of approach. Although I wasn't specifically talking about traveling, I was discussing how important awareness is and how it was actually possible for a civilian to understand, predict, and avoid critical areas, critical times, and their vulnerabilities. Also, I was discussing avenues of approach that attackers may take and that untrained civilians can actually pick that out as well if they understand how attackers think.

Several days later, Susan Googled my name and found that I had a public Facebook page. She emailed me, telling me her story about France and the gypsies. She was very interested in learning more about techniques to increase her awareness and abilities to predict where she would be a target. This couldn't have worked out any better because I had already started to write this book and was looking for case studies on awareness.

Susan and I spoke three times on the phone before she and her husband departed on a trip to the Philippines. The difference with this trip versus others was that they were not going alone, but with a small group of friends to celebrate a birthday. They had chosen the Philippines because one of their friends knew several people who lived there and had told them about how the group could take a moderately upscale trip without spending a lot of money. Because Susan and her husband would not be taking advantage of their high-level travelers' club, this was very inviting for them and their friends.

During the last conversation that Susan and I had one week before she departed, I sternly warned her to get out of the trip if possible as I had done some remote surveillance on the location that she was going to travel. Everything I looked up online concerning that area came with a stern warning of a rise in Islamic fundamentalist attacks. Also, the mode in which her group would be traveling from location to location (via small boat) was precisely the most likely target for kidnappings and violent attacks. Consequently, I gave her a set of instructions to build a target package on herself and their group by using information she could collect online. We discussed the U.S. State Department website (https://www.state.gov/travel/) as a good place to start, where she could get an idea of the threats that she might encounter. I explained that it would help guide her to a better understanding of an attacker's mindset particular to that region and the different areas she may be visiting. She was shocked with what she found! This was the official U.S. State Department warning about the exact areas they were traveling:

The Department of State warns U.S. citizens to avoid all non-essential travel to the Sulu Archipelago and through the southern Sulu Sea, and to exercise extreme caution when traveling to the island of Mindanao, due to continued terrorist threats, insurgent activities, and kidnappings.

She panicked, as would most people who were becoming aware of the dangers of the world around them. But for Susan, this was a stark realization because she knew that her husband and friends did not see things the way she did, and they would not want to cancel. So, Susan got busy. With my guidance, she began to develop a target package by following the steps listed in Chapters 3 and 4, dividing her entire trip into nine sectors that included:

- **Airport** (Departure)
- **Airport** (Arrival Manila)
- **Airport** (Arrival at forward location)
- **Trip to Island** (via boat)
- **Time at Island**
- **Trip Back to Airport** (Departure to Manila)
- **Airport** (Arrival Manila)
- **Hotel in Manila**
- **Airport** (Arrival in U.S.)

After Susan figured out the different sectors of her trip, she then divided each of the sectors into the five criticalities and proceeded to develop a picture of who, why, where, when, and how she could be attacked. She dove into the internet, researching everything she could find about the history (past and current events) related to the area that she would be traveling in.

Susan wanted to completely identify with the mindset of who might attack, and she wanted to know every detail about the trip and the environment that they would be traveling through.

Although apprehensive, Susan was comforted in knowing that she had put all the information together and determined the most likely areas that an attack could happen, as well as the locations and times where they would be most vulnerable. Now she felt as though she was as ready as she could be the day they left. Having developed a pretty good target package from an attacker's point of view, Susan then flipped the switch to defender and developed a package of things to take based on the types of attacks she could find herself in. Here's what her tactical loadout consisted of:

- High-powered but small flashlight
- Extra batteries
- GPS app for her phone
- Screenshots of maps of specific areas she'd be visiting and of vital contact information, plus printed, laminated backups of the maps and information in her purse
- Non-flashy clothes, purse, and accessories
- Male athletic tube socks and a typical combination lock that someone might use on a locker, both packed in the front pocket of her carry-on
- Sharp pair of tweezers
- Bug repellent

Regarding the socks and lock, Susan recalled a conversation we had and decided to carry something that could be used as a weapon. In case of an emergency, she would drop the lock into the socks and use it as a blunt-force object. The sharp pair of tweezers could also be used as an improvised weapon; however, the proximity to an attacker would have to be so dangerously close that they would most likely only be used as a last resort. Regardless, I liked the way Susan was starting to think in an offensive manner, using the attacker's mindset to set up defenses for potential violent encounters she could face.

Along with her tactical loadout, Susan made sure her medical vaccinations were up to date. (If you get taken hostage and you don't have current vaccinations, it's going to be a bad day.) She did her best to pack things separately, and she researched etymology issues common to the area in which she would be traveling. By this point, Susan was fluidly using the Attack and Defend technique, which led her to realize that not all attackers are human, hence the research on etymology issues in the Philippines. She realized they would be in a tropical setting and if something did happen and she had to escape and evade, she needed to know what critters were out there that could do her harm.

A few days before departing, Susan offered all this information to her husband and friends, but they laughed it off, thinking that because they were going to a "resort," they would have nothing to worry about.

They couldn't have been any more wrong!

Departing the Homeland

Finally, the day of departure had arrived. Upon arrival at the airport, one of their more charismatic male friends immediately started drinking. Before they even left the airport, this individual was drunk and attempting to sneak into first class so he could watch TV. Once the plane departed, he started drinking even more and got a bit out of control. The plane was packed, and the warning by staff did not go unnoticed by the majority of people on the flight. Already Susan could see where this was going, as they were now highlighted as drunk tourists on a plane to an area ripe with terrorists.

At the airport in Manila, Philippines, they waited for a connection to a smaller flight and their final destination. Despite what had happened on the plane with Susan's drunk friend, they were allowed to sit in a first-class area at the airport while they waited for their next flight.

Even though her research had given her a clear picture of the makeup of the population, Susan and her friends were surprised by the high Muslim population in the Philippines, and the rules and regulations that accompanied Muslim law. For instance, there were no bars in the airport, but there was a store that sold bottles of alcohol. So, despite Susan's planning, the entire group (including Susan) started drinking in the first-class lounge. *What could go wrong*, Susan thought to herself. *We are in an airport far away from the ticket counters where most airport shootings occur.* She had learned this from all her research on the internet before leaving.

That's when someone she had not planned on causing problems showed up—our old friend Murphy and his law. Susan had put so much emphasis in her planning on attacks by humans that she completely forgot about attacks by Mother Nature. That's when the storm hit.

Torrential rain and huge gusts of wind began pounding the airport. At one point, it got so bad that flights were being held from taking off or landing. Susan actually felt safer because, she figured, what terrorist would want to attack in such a storm? So she fully joined in the drinking and laughing, letting her guard down a bit more.

It was about that time when the roof of the first-class lounge they were sitting in was ripped completely off by the wind and the group found themselves sitting in the dark without a roof over their head in a torrential storm. BAM! Susan's awareness kicked back in as she dove into her purse for her flashlight. "Really," her friends laughed, "you have a high-speed flashlight in your purse?" The group quickly left the lounge and headed toward their gate, where the drinking came to an abrupt halt as they noticed there were a high number of Muslims waiting for the same flight. This was not expected, as their perception was the closer they got to their final destination, the more relaxed things would be. That did not seem to be the case.

Finally, their connecting flight arrived that would take them to the next-to-last stop. They would board this plane and, upon landing, take a nice boat ride to their final destination at the resort.

Upon arrival at the smaller airport, their group was huddled into a small area where they met their "handlers." One handler was especially odd-looking, with only a few teeth and extremely tattered clothing, and he was very insistent that he and the other handlers get their bags. This annoyed Susan and also made her suspect they might be up to something, if only searching for a tip (the trip was supposed to be all inclusive). The group was then made to wait until midnight for an armed Philippines Coast Guard vessel. They were not told why the Coast Guard would be the ones taking them to the island. All the tour guide kept saying was that it was because of weather, even though the weather had become clear and warm.

At midnight, the group was huddled onto the Coast Guard vessel for the final voyage to their island oasis. Armed guards crouched in what looked like fighting positions as Susan reflected on the lesson that Mother Nature had taught her at the airport. She sat next to the stairs, her eyes locked on the body language of the closest armed guard just above. Again, her friends were laughing and, believe it or not, drinking without a care in the world. At this point, Susan was actually glad she was so aware of what was going on, as it was almost like her own individual adventure. She knew, from her first visit to the State Department website, that the area they were in on that boat was probably the most dangerous part of the trip. However, the fact that they were on an armed Coast Guard vessel made her feel like this was the best possible way to venture through an area filled with bad guys.

When they arrived in the vicinity of the island, the Coast Guard vessel turned all its lights off and stopped about two hundred yards off shore. Floating in silence, one of the guards signaled toward shore with a small, white-light flashlight. Shortly after, a smaller boat came out and got the group, all under the cover of darkness with very little talking.

When they landed on shore, the staff greeted them and notified them that there was only one other family staying on the island. The staff member that briefed them also asked the group to please not tell the other family they had arrived that night because they didn't have a way to get them off the island at that time and didn't want to upset them. Susan thought to herself, *Is this an omen? Is this going to be the same problem we have when it's time to leave?*

Susan was not sure when the other group of guests finally departed the island, but during their stay, Susan and her group appeared to be the only people there, with the exception of the resort staff. The island was so small that there was only one resort. Despite the unbelievable trip that had taken place to get there, the resort staff put Susan at ease and the visit was uneventful. The only thing that was odd during their stay was the fact that they weren't allowed to go out into the ocean water, with the excuse again being "the weather" even though the weather was amazingly perfect.

Well, Susan thought, *if it doesn't get any worse than the trip here, we'll be fine.* And so she relaxed and drank, ate, and got sunburned like most people do on a tropical vacation.

I wish I could tell you this was the end of the story, but as Susan would tell you, "Hell no! Getting there was the easy part!"

Departing Paradise

After a week of fun in the sun, the group was ready to catch a flight the next day to Manila for a layover before their flight back to the United States. After they got packed and ready to leave, they ate dinner and planned to go to sleep so they could get up the next day and depart around noon. However, they soon discovered that it was their turn to not be let off the island like the family that was there when they had arrived. Again, the staff claimed they could not get a boat to take them off the island because of incoming bad weather, but as was always the case, the weather was perfect.

Susan was not having it and insisted to know what was really going on. However, she did not press the staff too hard and instead felt that politely engaging them was probably wise, as she didn't want to inflame whatever the situation was.

Susan calmly discussed the groups alternatives with the resort staff and was presented with two options:

1. The group could stay an extra day, rebook their flights ($1,000 each), and relax and drink on the house for another day.
2. The group could leave a bit earlier the next morning and board a speedboat owned by some locals that had volunteered to take them to the airport. The staff told them this trip would entail an "alternate route and some walking."

Susan's group refused to stay an extra day because they didn't want to pay extra money for tickets, so option two became the only option.

Because they insisted they wanted to leave on time, the staff got the group up at 5:00 a.m. and huddled them into a corner room, where they were somewhat isolated as they located the volunteer who was going to take them to the airport. Susan asked a staff member why they were being delayed and the staff member replied, "I can't say." So Susan asked the staff member that if *she* could get on this boat that was coming to get them, would she? The staff member once again stated, "I can't say." When the boat finally arrived, Susan's friends were already drunk and loud, without any idea about what was going on, as had been the case in every step of the trip so far.

When the group finally boarded the speedboat a few hours later, the sun was up and the weather couldn't have been any more perfect. Susan stayed in the corner of the boat in the front near the driver while her friends sat in the back acting loud and drunk. Out of the entire trip, Susan was now the most concerned because she was sober and very aware of how odd the entire situation was. She had done her research and understood that pirates and Islamic fighters were known to be in the area and as the boat departed, Susan vigorously scanned the water for any odd boats that might be in the vicinity. After some time on the open ocean, their boat slowed and turned up the mouth of a river. At first it was just desolate jungle on each shore and as they progressed ever further up the river, the smaller it got with more and more trash floating around them. Eventually they started to see shanty homes with pigs and livestock eating out of the trash in the river. Susan noticed the sewer running into the river. *This can't be a good sign*, she thought. Everything was mixed together—sewage, waste, and domesticated animals. It was awful.

It was now 8:00 a.m., and the people on shore were starting to notice the boat as they passed, mainly because her friends were making so much noise and because a speedboat was probably not what they normally saw driving up the river.

The staff members at the hotel had told them before they left to wear sneakers, long-sleeve shirts, and long pants because they would be walking through a town with lots of mosquitos. Susan was starting to worry that it was not the mosquitos they were going to have a problem with. She noticed the indigenous people on shore were very poor and possibly Muslim. (Many of the Muslims in that area did not wear traditional garb but still did not take well to scantily clad women.) She saw no women, few kids, and almost all men standing on the shores as they passed by. Susan described herself as being dressed like a beekeeper, while her friends were dressed for the beach with revealing clothes. And yes, they were still drinking.

Eventually the boat docked on the edge of the river, and one of the volunteers gestured for them to follow him. The group got out of the boat one by one and walked down a mud path that led through a small village. Everyone was staring at them, and as Susan had noticed before, it was almost all men. The looks they received were not comforting at all to Susan, with intense stares that made it seem as if the locals were contemplating kidnapping the group. Susan was trying to find the middle-ground between rational thought and delusions brought on by a feeling of panic. But because she had thought about all these types of scenarios before leaving the United States, she felt like she was ready to act if the time arose.

One of the men in her group began to draw major attention to himself by asking the locals if he could buy food from them so he could feed the dogs they were passing along the way. His behavior was, from what Susan could tell, very rude, and while he was having fun, the faces of the residents were not reflecting the same emotion.

Finally, after about an hour, the group passed through the town. When they arrived at the main road, there was a bus waiting for them that had been sent by the island staff.

When Susan boarded the bus, she immediately noticed that the bus driver was the same guy (toothless with tattered clothing) who had handled their luggage when they arrived. Believe it or not, this made her feel somewhat comforted because he was a familiar face. Yes, a gummy, toothless smile can be a sight for sore eyes.

The bus, driven by the toothless helper, took them straight to the airport where they would catch the flight that would take them to Manila.

Upon arrival in Manila, the group planned to go out because they only had one night there. They were staying in Makati, which is like the Beverly Hills of Manila.

The hotel was like a palace, with floor-to-ceiling marble. However, before the group was allowed to enter the premises, they had to be sniffed by dogs. She didn't know if it was drug dogs or bomb dogs, but, either way, it was odd.

After getting settled in her room, the last thing Susan wanted to do was party. She was not feeling good and did not want to go out that night because of the stress from the trip. However, she agreed to go eat dinner with the group across the street.

When they left the hotel to go to the restaurant, one of the hotel security guards shadowed them across the street because, regardless of the impressive hotel and upper-class location, it was still that dangerous. *Damn*, Susan thought, *is there any place that I can let my guard down in this country?*

When they arrived back at their hotel, Susan excused herself and went back to the room while her husband and friends went out partying with locals, which included a stop at the Resorts World Manila Hotel and Casino where sixty people were killed on June 1, 2017, after a robber (who suspiciously used tactics identical to a terrorist) entered with a rifle and set the building on fire before killing himself.

The next day, Susan and all her friends (who were suffering from severe hangovers) departed the Philippines for the long plane ride back to the United States. Susan was now extremely excited to be heading home, away from the constant threat of kidnapping and/or death.

Unfortunately, one thing Susan did not anticipate was catching a parasite. She has since been plagued with gastrointestinal issues and is unable to eat meat-based proteins without getting severely ill.

Let's just say, bad choices can affect you for a lifetime. But as Susan exclaimed, at least she still has her life to live. Even if it's with a tiny parasitic friend.

Conclusion

ATTACK AND DEFEND is a seed that is now planted inside your consciousness and subconsciousness, enabling you to understand the basic threats and high-threat areas in and around your life. As I said in the beginning of this book, Attack and Defend is aimed at civilians as a target audience, not security experts. Ultimately, you, not the authorities, are going to protect you, secure your home, increase your awareness, and get you out of a dangerous situation. Police and firefighters are not going to teach you this, and they are not going to guide you home late at night to your walk-up apartment or secure your surroundings when you're at work or in school. Public servants are only slightly proactive and rely heavily on hopefully quick reactions and responses to situations.

September 11, 2001, is a date that we all remember, and it is etched in history as a reminder of how a lack of awareness and understanding of attack planning and tactical evolution can have grand impacts on every walk of life. The authorities were not able to stop 9/11 from happening, largely in part because they did not think a plan like that was possible. They relied on the historical statistics (probabilities) that said if planes were hijacked, they would simply land and ask for something, or demand that the plane be flown to a specific location. Even though terrorist activity had increased and become more destructive leading up to 9/11, the people charged to protect you were basically asleep at the wheel. Really? Is that possible?

Well, fast-forward sixteen years and return to the same World Trade Center area in lower Manhattan. The new Freedom Tower now stands 1,776 feet above the sprawling area that was rebuilt in place of the Twin Towers. While the building was being built, there were no fewer than four trespassing incidents through security perimeters, three of which were made through the same gaping hole in the fencing around the property. In the first case, a sixteen-year-old boy was able to sneak through the hole in the fence and convince an elevator operator that he was supposed to be there. The boy was then able to get to the top of the Freedom Tower and take several pictures of himself before coming back down and eventually being arrested. A few weeks later, two CNN reporters made it through the same hole that had not been fixed and were subsequently arrested. A week later, pictures of a sleeping security guard at the same area were plastered all over the press, as was a video released by trespassers as they climbed to the top of the building and parachuted off. What does this tell you? It tells you that a lot of security (even in and around the biggest terrorist bullseye in the world) is still merely ineffectual smoke and mirrors.

Knowing this, you should realize that the same goes for safety in and around your community and home. "To protect and to serve" is the motto of a lot of police agencies. However, that should actually be changed to, "to respond and sometimes be there as it happens." I say this in all seriousness and with no malice toward law enforcement. The fact is, police and first responders can only be in so many places at one time. And unfortunately, the widespread plague of incompetent leadership in law enforcement and other first-responder units has swept across the country faster than a jet airplane. When you combine these two huge truths, you can see clear avenues of approach as well as critical areas that can be exploited. Just like the sixteen-year-old that performed surveillance on the Freedom Tower complex to gain access to the top of the building, bad guys will also perform surveillance and exploit weaknesses to carry out an attack. If you understand your surroundings and apply the technique of Attack and Defend taught in this book, it will be of no surprise to you when people around you are up to no good. You will understand what's normal and what's not in all aspects of your life.

The technique of Attack and Defend can work with a facility or even an entire city as well as it does a single person. Imagine if everyone in a city understood why, where, when, and how an attack could happen. Police would be better positioned for reaction and, in many cases, actually positioned for action. Facilities like stadiums and arenas would have a more robust security force because, literally, every person who worked or attended events would function as a force multiplier for their security, and they would act instead of react in the cases where an attack actually did happen. Kids would be safer because they would attend schools that actually had a grasp of the daily threats. Their field trips would be better planned and carried out in a safer fashion, and all the eyes would function as force multipliers for the staff.

Yes, it is that easy! You don't need fancy charts or matrix diagrams. You don't need FBI Special Agents, Navy SEALs, or any other "security experts" taking your money to tell you what you already know. Now that you have the same tactical understanding as an attacker who wants to exploit your critical areas, critical times, vulnerabilities, and avenues of approach, you are just as knowledgeable as the experts and in fact more knowledgeable than anyone who wants to harm you.

Awareness is the key, and if you choose to apply this awareness in your everyday life proactively, you will see that there is practically no reason you should ever find yourself caught up in an actual surprise attack. Apply these proven proactive awareness techniques to your life and I promise, like Cleo and her friends on vacation, you will be able to avoid the critical areas when you can and develop highly effective, proactive plans of action to act, not just react, when destiny calls.

One Last Prediction

LET ME LEAVE YOU with one last prediction of an attack that has both high probability as well as an absolute possibility. Based on my targeting and analysis, utilizing the Attack and Defend technique, Times Square in the heart of New York City will see a future attack by Fundamental Islamic attackers. The Attack and Defend target equation is as follows:

Sector

- **TIMES SQUARE**
  - *Most Critical Areas*
    - —Large seating area on the northwest side of Times Square between 47th Street and 46th Street
    - —Large seating area on the southeast side of Times Square between 42nd Street and 43rd Street
  - *Attackers' Avenues of Approach*
    - —Straight down 7th Avenue
    - —Across 47th, 46th, 45th, 44th, and 43rd Streets
  - *The Sum of Sector TIMES SQUARE's Target Equation*
    - —Type of Attack
      - ○ Time of Attack
        - · Vulnerabilities

—VBIED
- Between 12 p.m.–10 p.m.
- Friday, Saturday, and Sunday
- Spring, summer, and fall see highest numbers of tourists, with greatest number from June through August
  - The highly congested 7th Avenue and the busy cross streets are consistently packed with automobiles of all sizes, including personal vehicles, taxis, full-size buses, and large construction trucks
  - The Seating areas create a bottleneck of patrons and visitors where thousands of people linger for extended periods of time
  - The Broadway ticket area along with the large bleacher section are extreme bottlenecks for tourists

—Mass Shooting/Mass Stabbings
- Between 12 p.m.–10 p.m.
- Friday, Saturday, and Sunday
- Spring, summer, and fall see highest numbers of tourists, with greatest number from June through August
  - Included with the vulnerabilities above, the crowd is so densely populated on warm spring, summer, and fall weekends that police will not be able to adequately move through the crowd if multiple shooters are involved and the crowd is surging

—Vehicle Attack Possibly Followed by Possible Stabbings or Shootings
   - Between 12 p.m.–10 p.m.
   - Friday, Saturday, and Sunday
   - Spring, summer, and fall see highest numbers of tourists, with greatest number from June through August
     - Included with the vulnerabilities above, the crowd is so densely populated on warm spring, summer and fall weekends that they often press to the edge of the cross streets at the busier intersections at 47th, 46th, 45th, 44th, and 43rd Streets

While most people would probably think that New Year's Eve in Times Square is the busiest, the threat is mitigated because the area is locked down to pedestrian traffic only during the time leading up to the celebration. On the day of the actual celebration for New Year's Eve, the entire area is frozen and people are searched before entering the frozen zone. Summer days have no frozen zones and people are allowed to congregate anywhere and for as long as they want, making the soft target areas more densely populated and for a longer time while remaining unprotected.

Please share this prediction and your new knowledge gained through this book with as many people as you possibly can, and remember: fear is not a gift anyone needs. Awareness is the true gift you can give yourself, and it's a gift you can share with others, exponentially increasing safety and literally saving lives. One Team, One Fight!

TRUTH HAS ARRIVED!

About the Author

Jonathan T. Gilliam is a career public servant with over twenty years of service as a Navy SEAL, FBI Special Agent, Federal Air Marshal, Private Security Contractor, Police Officer, Public Speaker, Expert Media Commentator, and Host of The EXPERTS, broadcast on Facebook, Twitter, and YouTube. Gilliam has extensive experience in crisis management, threat analysis and mitigation, small unit leadership, on-scene command, and special events/crisis management.

NOTES

NOTES

NOTES

NOTES

NOTES

NOTES

NOTES